Joy Comes in the Morning

Hopolang Phororo

MKUKI NA NYOTA
DAR-ES-SALAAM

PUBLISHED BY
Mkuki na Nyota Publishers Ltd
Nyerere Road, Quality Plaza Building
P. O. Box 4246
Dar es Salaam, Tanzania
www.mkukinanyota.com
publish@mkukinanyota.com

© Hopolang Phororo, 2011

First edition 2005

ISBN 1-4141-0498-7

Published in 2005 by Pleasant Word
(a division of WinePress Publishing, P.O. Box 428, Enumclaw, WA 98022)

Second Edition 2011

ISBN 978-9987-08-153-0

All rights reserved. No part of this publication may be reproduced, stored in a retrieval system or transmitted in any form or by any means, electronic, mechanical, photocopying, recording, or otherwise, without the prior permission of the Mkuki na Nyota Pulishers

This book is sold subject to the condition that it should not by way of trade or otherwise be lent, re-sold, hire out or otherwise circulated without the publisher's prior consent in any form of binding or cover other than that in which it is published and without a similar condition including this condition being imposed on the subsequent purchaser.

We have been unable to trace the copyright holders of the cover image (leaping lady) and we would appreciate any information that would enable us to do so. We would be pleased to insert the appropriate acknowledgement in subsequent reprints.

CHAPTER ONE

∽ 1 ∾

CHAPTER TWO

∽ 13 ∾

CHAPTER THREE

∽ 20 ∾

CHAPTER FOUR

∽ 29 ∾

CHAPTER FIVE

∽ 40 ∾

CHAPTER SIX

∽ 61 ∾

CHAPTER SEVEN

∽ 89 ∾

CHAPTER EIGHT

∽ 127 ∾

CHAPTER NINE

∽ 149 ∾

TO ALL MY "DAUGHTERS OF DESTINY"

This book is dedicated to all my Daughters of Destiny, wherever you are... Thank you for giving me the privilege to learn so much from you as you opened your hearts and lives to me. You girls are so special. I know that you can be all that God has called you to be. Use your gifts to be the best that you can be and the change that you want to see happen. Never settle for less and set your minds on God's standards of excellence. Remember that with Him, all things are possible. And always remember that as you have received, so you can give. It was He, "who comforts me in all my troubles, so that I can comfort those in any trouble with the comfort I myself have received from God. For just as the sufferings of Christ flow over into my life, so also through Christ my comfort overflows".

(paraphrased, 2 Corinthians 1:4-5, NIV)

ACKNOWLEDGEMENTS

I give thanks to the Lord who, even before I was conceived in my mother's womb, knew what He had planned for me. He knew that through the painful experience of sexual abuse I would overcome and be able to testify to His faithfulness and His goodness. He who makes no mistakes knew what I had to go through to become the woman that I am today. I marvel as His purposes unfold in my life and I know that the best is yet to come. Glory to God!

I am forever grateful to the parents that the Lord blessed me with. I give tribute to my late beloved Dad, whose memory I cherish. It has been some years, Mom since I told you about being sexually abused. Thanks for understanding me and accepting me, and for being available always. I love you.

Chips and Lefo, thank you for putting up with me, even when I have said and done things that hurt you at times. It was never intentional and you know that I want the very best for you. You know what I have gone through and what a journey it has been... I am a work in progress. I am grateful to your spouses, who might have never quite understood me but were always supportive of my relationship with you.

My appreciation and gratitude goes to Sister Diane from Kingdom Faith Builders Ministries Inc. for introducing me to the Daughters in Namibia. Thanks for inviting me to share my story and for embracing me as part of a special ministry for young women. This was where I discovered my passion and my own ministry. Thanks to you and Bishop Abraham Wahl for remembering and keeping me in your prayers.

I give thanks to the Lord for the pastors and their spouses who have sowed spiritually in my life and who taught me— Mama and Ntate Moledi from Faith Tumelo Ministries, Pastor Roy and Gerda Wallace from Gospel Outreach, Pastor Tunde and Sister Bose from International Pentecostal Church, Pastor Carl and Patricia Shipley from Redeemed Church of Christ— Geneva, Martin and Margaret Emmerson, and Doug and Lyndi Buckley from Vineyard. Thank you for what you deposited in my spirit because that is what kept and continues to keep me focused. Thank you for believing in me, and for your prayers and support for the Daughters of Destiny Ministry.

If I were to start naming the friends and sisters who have blessed me in so many ways and have sowed so much into my life, I would never finish. But, you know who you are. Thank you for believing in me, for praying for me and the Daughters of Destiny Ministry, for crying with me, for laughing with me and above all, for accepting me, even when I was at my worst.

So many other people have touched my life; some of them don't even know that they did. I am the person I am because of the footprints that you left and I am so grateful for that.

I am thankful to Pleasant Word Publishing for publishing the first edition of Joy Comes in the Morning. My thanks go to Tapiwa Muchechemera of Mkuki na Nyota, who believed a market exists for Joy Comes in the Morning in East Africa and encouraged me to update and to come up with a revised edition. Thank you so much, Warren Reed for editing the revised chapters; you really helped me with your probing questions, as I uncovered what I had within me. It was a process but a great delight to see the final product.

I

As I walked in front of them, their eyes turned toward me—some with smiles on their faces and others wearing indifferent looks. I knew that they had been told about me and were expecting me to visit and to share my story with them. My audience was young women ranging in age from thirteen to twenty-five years. Some of them worked and others attended school or university. These were the Daughters of Destiny, who were struggling with challenges such as various forms of abuse and rejection from parents or other family members. Most of the young women were Christians.

I looked at the young women and I felt that I shared something with them. I was excited and felt drawn to them. Questions coursed through my mind: *Would they listen to me? What did they think about me?* As I looked at them, I could sense the discouragement and the pain and the turmoil and in others an attitude of "Let's hear what she has to say that is different from others."

I took a deep breath. I was determined to go on, as I remembered how long I had waited for this moment. This was a dream come true. I was convinced that this was what the Lord had called me to do—to comfort young women who had gone through experiences like my own. I had overcome; therefore, my message was that there was hope also for them. I knew that what I had to say would touch a life in that room, because someone in the audience needed to hear my story.

As I started, I noted from the expressions on their faces that I had their attention.

No major or earth-shattering events are associated with the year of my birth, but definitely in the life of one young woman who was born in what used to be Umtali, Rhodesia, it was a major event. This was her second delivery in a country far away from her own, and it must have been quite an experience. Thank God she could count on my dad's support. Two days before Christmas and two weeks before the due date, a baby was born in Queen Elizabeth II Hospital in Maseru, Lesotho, which was at that time called Basotholand. The healthy but small baby girl was named "Hopolang," which means, "to remember," by her paternal grandfather. I was twelve months younger than my older sister, and many times she would spank me. I guess that was sister rivalry; maybe she was not impressed with this addition to the family so soon after her own birth.

While I was growing up, I would ask my mom why I had not been born in Northern Ireland like my older sister. I felt cheated, and I did not understand why my parents had not stayed in Europe longer, because there was no glamour associated with my being born in Lesotho. I had to accept my birthplace since there was nothing I could do to change the situation. I don't remember much about my childhood days, except that I loved drawing, reading, collecting bits and pieces, and doing schoolwork. My nursery teacher would often tell my parents that I was smart and that gave them great pleasure. I had friends at pre-school, and I went all the way up to the later years of primary school with them, and to this day, I am still communicating with some of them.

We welcomed a third addition to the family, my younger brother, who is fifteen months younger than I am, and, indeed, in an African family, a boy is a delight as the heir to the throne. I got on well with him and I did not spank him. I was darker in complexion than my siblings, and the relatives had a nickname for me, which some still use to this day. It is *Mantso*, which means "the black one." Of course, at that tender age, I began to have a complex because this nickname was derogatory, and dark-skinned people were not perceived as good looking. My mother used to hate that name and protested it being used because she knew what damage it would cause. My uncle also called me *Ma-likatane*, which means "the rubbish lady," because I was always collecting bits and pieces.

I sucked my thumb until I was about thirteen years old, and until I was about six years, I wet my bed. My parents tried all the tricks to get me to stop sucking my thumb, but this was to no avail. I stopped when I licked an ice cube from the ice tray and my tongue got stuck on it. As I tried to pull it away, I cut my tongue, and it was too painful to suck my thumb, so that was the end of that. What a relief for everyone.

I grew up in a middle-class family, so with Mom being from Zimbabwe and Dad from Lesotho, English was the language that was spoken in the house. We spoke Sesotho, but since Mom did not speak it fluently, it was easier to speak English, but Dad would occasionally speak Sesotho to us. The relatives did not take too well to the fact that we were not fluent in Sesotho. They referred to us as *Makhoatsoana*, which means "the little white ones," and as a result, we were never considered to be a part of them. To make matters worse, we attended English primary schools and that put us into another league. We learned how to swim at a young age, since we had a big swimming pool in the garden, and when we were older, Mom sent us for ballet and piano lessons. Unfortunately, we did not persevere and gave up sooner rather than later. Mom wanted to give us the opportunities that she had never had as a child, and we cannot say she did not try. Like a true mother, she made several sacrifices so that we could have the best upbringing.

She was a stay-at-home mom and would sew our clothes, cushion covers, curtains, and whatever else she could find. She also knitted and was a real homemaker. She went back to work only when my brother started primary school. At school, we were the laughingstock because we wore homemade clothes and other children taunted us for being poor. However, we never said that we were rich, and we would not pay much attention to it because there was never a night that we would go without food. We could not afford luxuries because my parents were building a house, and there were times when the going was tough. They told us that, so we knew we could not get whatever we wanted.

Dad owned a farm, and on weekends, we would all go to the farm, particularly during planting season to plant potatoes. It was hard work, but for us children it was fun. However, we observed and learned from that young age that, in order to succeed in life, you had to work hard, and my parents were a living testimony to that. We were not spoilt, and my mother taught us the importance of being humble and never to look down on anyone. She told us that we were all different, with some who were better off than others, but that was not a license to be proud. So, all the house helpers were like family members and we never looked down on them. We had to assist with household chores, and there was no lazing around because someone would pick up after us.

When Mom joined the labor force, we saw Mom and Dad only at lunchtime and in the evenings. In the meantime, Dad was progressing in his career and that placed immense pressure on him. He was so busy, and as he provided for his family, time spent together as a family was rare. He would also travel frequently, and, of course, when he returned from the trips, like most children, we would be more excited to see what he had brought for us than to see him. He always brought us wonderful gifts that we truly treasured. Dad worked hard because he wanted to ensure that the family was well provided for, but in the meantime, we lost the opportunity to get closer to him. This is a trend that is so common in many middle-class African families, where, as the fathers are busy providing for the family, they do not bond with the children. There is no quality time spent with the children because the father works so hard and is exhausted by the time he gets home. It's a shame, and many times the bonding takes place between the mother and the children and the father is almost a stranger to his own children.

One great thing in our family was that the concept of holidays was learned at a young age, and we would often travel to Zimbabwe by road to visit Mom's family. It was always an adventure, because en route through South Africa, we would have to sleep along the roadside in the car. It was the 1970s, and blacks were not allowed to stay in hotels. It was only later that we were afforded that privilege. I remember the time we had an orange VW Combie and we were en route to Zimbabwe where we slept along the roadside. We had a watermelon in the back of the Combie, which was open. As some cows passed by one morning, they gobbled up all the melon. We children were so horrified that these cows had the audacity to eat our watermelon, but it was a relief that another could be purchased! These holidays exposed us to different places and cultures and made us different from a lot of children in that we became broadminded, unlike our friends, who did not have such privileges, since both of their parents were from Lesotho.

We used to get a fixed sum of pocket money, but Mom taught us to be very enterprising if we wanted extra to purchase something. We would give the children in the neighborhood our bicycle and they paid for rides. We would also sell peaches and apples from the farm. Our peers thought our folks were being hard on us, but again, this was a lesson of life being imparted to us. To the contrary, we had lots of fun and never felt that our parents were mean.

Even at a young age, the signs of a great leader were eminent in me, because many times I'd convince my siblings to do what I deemed important. They used to think I was bossy. I remember one day we wanted some sweets, but we did not have enough money and did not want to ask Mom because we got pocket money. So, I told my siblings that if we went into the house helper's room through the window, we could get some money. My sister, being the biggest physically, had to be the ladder, and my brother, being the smallest, could squeeze in through the window. So we hoisted him up and forgot to check his feet to make sure that they were clean. He got in and came out with few cents, and we were able to buy the sweets.

Later, when the house helper came from her afternoon visit, she reported to Mom that someone had gone into her room through the window and there were small footprints on her white bedspread. Mom called the three of us and we knew that we were in serious trouble. How could we have been so stupid and not checked our brother's feet? Mom asked who had done such a terrible thing. My sister and brother pointed at me and said, "Hopolang said that we should go in...." Of course, I refused to accept the blame and passed it to my younger brother. My mom had got tired of hearing "Hopolang said..." and chastised my older sister. Being the eldest, she should have refused, but instead, she had been swayed and agreed to commit such an awful act. After that, the three of us got a good thrashing, and that was the last time that we went into the house helper's room looking for money.

We had a lot of fun playing with the next-door neighbor's children who were about the same age as we were. Our neighbors were from Uganda and though our parents did not meet often, we children had a good relationship. We would visit with the neighbor's children, and they would visit with us. Their father took us for picnics into the beautiful mountains of Lesotho. It was refreshing and awesome. He purchased sweets, chips, and all those treats children love. Summer days, especially the holidays, were lovely, because we could be outside playing for long hours since it got dark late.

During weekdays, we were busy with school activities and homework. School was not a problem for me, and I was in the top ten percent of the class. I did not have a boyfriend, but I did fancy one boy. One holiday, when we went to the mountains, I was ecstatic when I heard this boy was also going to be there. However, he never did ask me out, but still I was head over heels in love with him. My other girlfriends often teased me. The saddest time for me was when he left Lesotho for good, and I was never to see or hear from him again.

On one specific day, I went to the neighbor's house to play with the children, and just before I entered the house, the father asked me to get into the car. I did not ask any questions and just assumed that we were going to the shops or for a ride. The details I cannot recall. However, what I remember is that we went through the same motions of purchasing chips and sweets as though we were going for a picnic, even though the other children were not around. I learned later that our neigbour had been a soldier in Idi Amin's government and was the type of man you did not ask questions. Even in his own house he was feared, and the children, especially his oldest son, did not dare get in his way. He had four children—three boys and a girl—and his wife's sister also lived with him and his wife. The wife's sister was a really nice girl. She taught me to plait cornrows and I perfected the skill. I started practicing on my dolls, and by the time I was fourteen, I was plaiting people's hair and earning some pocket money. I even designed a hairstyle book and just loved to experiment with fancy styles. I was creative and even with the bits and pieces I collected, and I could put them to good use.

Anyway, let me get back to the story. We drove out of town, in the direction of the usual picnic spots. At this time, I was getting rather frightened because it did not seem like any of the other children or my siblings were joining us; but still, I asked no questions. Then he turned off the main road and went to a cluster of trees, a place that I can still identify, and stopped the car. He offered me a drink, and, to be honest with you, I don't remember all the details, but I recall him opening the glove box and there I saw a gun. Of course, that was very traumatic, and then he proceeded to sexually abuse me. I did not understand what was happening when he penetrated me and then made some strange noises. Then it was all over. After that, he gave me something and we drove home. I must have been in total shock, because I don't remember what he gave me, and anything that happened after that I cannot recall. But I did not utter a word to anyone and retreated into my shell. I became very frightened of everything, and going anywhere on my own was a terrifying experience. I became withdrawn and my confidence and creativity died after that experience.

I continued going to visit the neighbor's children with my siblings. I remember times when I would go to the toilet and he would waylay me and push me into the bathroom and proceed to abuse me. Any opportunity he had he sexually abused me, and this went on for a year. Even when we moved from the house where we were staying, he continued to stalk me. He maintained contact with my parents and gave the impression that he respected the family, and yet he sexually abused me. How ironic that was! I remember that, on certain days after school, he would drive by the house, and I knew he was looking for me. I felt that if I did not go out, he would do something terrible—the gun was something that haunted me. I wondered what he would do if I told my parents. Suppose he killed them!

His family returned to Uganda, and from what we heard, he was wanted in Uganda. He was a man on the run and did not stay in one place. He even wanted Dad to get him out of the country, but Dad did not want to get involved in that. He would still continue to drive past the house, and I would tell the house helper I was going for a walk, then he would pick me up and sexually abuse me. Even when I was visiting with friends he seemed to know where to find me, and even then I had to try so hard to pretend to my friends that there was nothing going on. That was not easy. At least, he was cautious enough to use condoms so that I would not get pregnant. He seemed to be obsessed with me, and that was really difficult, for he always seemed to show up where I was.

I blamed myself for what was happening, and since this had been going on for so long I did not know how I could explain it. I was not sure who would believe me, and maybe I was the one who had encouraged him, so it was a burden I would have to carry. That was one very heavy burden—with devastating consequences.

I remember that every time after he had abused me, I took a bath and washed myself with a stone to cleanse myself, but I still felt so dirty. I remember trying to tell my sister what had happened, but she did not seem to understand, so I let it be. I guess a fifteen-year-old girl is not able to understand the whole issue of her younger sister being sexually abused. I kept silent. Who could I tell? Who would understand? At school, I withdrew into my shell, and when my friends began to date guys, I did not see myself as worthy to be dated. I used to believe that boys would see straight through me. My self-esteem was stripped from me, and I told myself the guys would never look at me because I was ugly.

While this was happening, Mom and Dad did not see that their daughter was going through so much. They were so busy advancing in their careers and ensuring that we were well provided for. Then Dad got a job in Italy, and we all moved from Lesotho. That was such a welcome change because, with that, the abuse stopped. I was already so damaged.

II

Going to Rome was an adventure, but I don't recall ever being happy about anything again. Nothing excited me, and instead, I felt so tired and so old. That carefree spirit was gone, and I guess just the sheer weight of the burden that I was carrying and could not share with anyone was too much. The good thing about going to Rome was that Mom was there for us all the time, and we bonded as a family. There was no longer that pressure on them to work so hard, and we went for family outings and holidays. They were fun, but for me, never like the holidays we had taken to Zimbabwe.

I decided one thing and that was to excel at school and be the best that I could be. I knew that if I excelled, no one could take that away from me. I would get approval. I thought that then I would feel better. I was a serious student and did well in school, until I got to A Levels.[1] A racist teacher gave me F and D+ grades for Economics, and, so naturally, I failed the course. That lowered my self-esteem further, and I started to believe that I was useless. When Dad also expressed his disappointment in the bad grades, after my having done so well in O levels, that didn't help, and I pushed myself further to prove to him that I was not stupid but that I was smart. When I enrolled in an American college, I got straight As, and, in addition, I was on the dean's list. I had proved a point and felt that at least Dad could respect me. But the feelings of worthlessness never went away, no matter how much I tried to get approval. I was always falling short.

When my brother got annoyed with me, he would tell me that my legs were like "split poles," ugly and shapeless. Since my self-esteem was so low, I believed him and figured that no one should see my legs. So I hid them and wore trousers most of the time. When I wore skirts or dresses I was so self-conscious. I really believed that my legs were ugly. As I grew older and wore skirts or dresses, I received many compliments but never believed them. It is only in recent years that I have come to the point of accepting myself as I am. My style of dressing was very conservative: dark colors, nothing revealing, and with my legs covered. I did not want to attract attention and preferred to get by unnoticed. I did not know how to receive compliments, and so it was better for me to "blend into the woodwork."

---

[1] In the British system, after 4 years of high school, students write O Levels and then after an additional two years, students write A Levels. Thereafter they proceed to university.

When Mom wanted to send me to the stores alone to purchase bread or milk, I would refuse, almost to the point of crying. I could not go out there on my own. I kept thinking, what if someone sexually abused me? Mom did not understand; she just thought I was extremely shy and encouraged me to go. I finally would have to go, and what an ordeal it would be. I was so terrified.

Also, when Mom, Dad, or my siblings showed affection toward me, I would visibly freeze. They did not understand and never pursued the matter further. They thought that it was strange.

Dad started jogging and the whole family followed suit. We participated in many races and would do very well, even taking a few trophies home. Later, when I started dealing with my past, I saw that I jogged to keep fit and shapely so that I would be attractive. I wanted so much to be loved, and this was one way I thought it could be achieved. I heard people say that I had a good body, and to me that excluded my legs and my face. So I decided that I would keep fit. In addition, I felt that my body had betrayed me by responding to the man who had sexually abused me. I wondered why I had responded, so I thought running would be a kind of punishment I could inflict on my body.

Interestingly, I made friends with girls quite easily, and I had a Nigerian friend, who is still a very special friend as I write this story. Girls seemed harmless to me until they started to show affection or compliment me, but that was not a major problem. Making friends with boys was such a challenge. I felt that they wanted sex and so I kept far from them. I went to parties together with my friend, and she had many boyfriends. I envied her because I knew that I could not have a boyfriend.

We had many parties when we were in Rome. Mom and Dad encouraged us to host them at home. They would go out for the night, and when they returned in the early hours of the morning, the party would be over. They did not want to be too strict with us and felt that if they refused to let us to have parties we would do worse things. So, they gave us that opportunity. Dancing at those parties, particularly to slow music, was so difficult for me. I would freeze in the guy's arms, and when he started getting fresh and wanted a kiss, I would get away from him as quickly as possible.

I remember one guy I really liked, and when I was in his arms dancing, he asked me why I was so "frozen" and told me to relax. What do I have to do to relax? I wondered, because I didn't know what it was like to relax. I was constantly tense, and for me that was fine, because it enabled me to be vigilant, just in case someone wanted to hurt me. Needless to say, nothing came out of the relationships with all those guys who were potential boyfriends. To me it was just proof that I was ugly and that no one wanted to date me anyway.

After eight and a half years in Rome, we had to return to Lesotho since Dad had been recalled by the late Majesty King Moshoeshoe II to serve in government. We were not too thrilled about going back home. Luckily for my brother and me, we were proceeding on to the United States of America to continue our studies, whereas, my sister chose to go to Zimbabwe. During those eight and half years in Italy, we visited Brussels, Paris, London, and various parts of Italy. Those visits were memorable. We made a lot of friends in Rome, and, fortunately for me, my Nigerian girlfriend and I decided that we would apply to the same universities and ultimately go to the same one.

We returned to Lesotho before going to the US, but the friends we had prior to going to Italy had gone their own ways, and we found we did not quite fit into the scheme of things there. However, my time in Lesotho was brief. Leaving the security of home was a very painful experience for me. I remember crying so much when I bid goodbye to Mom at the airport. I could not imagine being so far away from Mom. She was also sad, and you would have thought she knew what kind of suffering I was going through. Even though my brother was going to be in the US, it was just frightening, but thank God I was going to be with my friend.

I headed to Duquesne University in the US, and deep down I hoped that things would be better over there. But that did not happen, because I had not dealt with the past. I fell into the same traps of not being able to relate with guys. One type of male I despised was a married man. I loathed them, and when a married man spoke to me, I'd be so rude and defensive. I built up walls around myself and kept far from them. Even with the single ones, I only allowed them so far and then I'd be so unreasonable that they would see there was no point in going further with me. They'd ditch me and I'd console myself with, "I expected that because men are useless anyway and who needs one?" My girlfriend, in the meantime, had many boyfriends, so she would be busy with dates, and I would stay in the room and cry myself to sleep, wondering what was wrong with me. I would then delve into my work and try to forget the misery I was in. I started wondering if I would ever truly be happy in life.

However, no one thought there was anything wrong with me, because I socialized. When there were outings, such as picnics, dinners, and parties, I would go and have fun. I would chat with classmates and have a good laugh, but it was all a life of pretence, because deep down I was not a happy person. I envied the couples that were in love and watched them from a distance, hoping that one day I would get to that point. Even if there were guys around me who wanted to ask me out, I gave them vibes that I was not interested in men but rather in my studies or I was generally unapproachable. I did not want to be alone with any guy. What if he sexually abused me? I did not have the strength to be abused again, so life went on.

After being in the States for four months, I met a guy I liked, and he liked me, so we dated for about a year, my longest relationship. We got on really well, and since he lived in another city, he would drive long distances to spend time with me. To go to so much trouble to see me made me feel loved and appreciated. However, the past was still buried in my subconscious, and I would not entertain opening up Pandora's box. So, I did not really open up to him because I did not trust him and his intentions.

Certain events highlighted my loneliness, even when I was in the midst of people. I met a young lady from the Bahamas and she invited me to visit her. I took up the offer and ventured out on the first adventure of my life on my own and landed in Nassau. What a beautiful island to be visiting! Since she was dating someone who doted on her, I felt that it was a shame to have no special man in my life. I also remember going to Anita Baker and Luther Vandross concerts when I was in Pittsburgh, and I felt so sad when I got back to the dorms because there was no one special in my life. It was a really tough time for a twenty-three year-old girl. When everyone is dating and you are not, it appears as though there is something wrong with you, which was the case for me.

III

I left the states after graduating and went back to Lesotho. My sister got married and I felt happy for her. My relationship with my boyfriend continued, and when I left, we had been dating for a year. I kept in touch with him, and then we lost contact since we did not know when we would meet again. So that was very painful for me, and I just occupied myself with work in Lesotho. I tried to fit into the Maseru crowds, but it was not easy. I no longer shared anything in common with old friends, so I had to strike up new friendships. In addition, Dad was now the minister of agriculture, so people tended to put me on a pedestal and did not get to know me. I ended up feeling quite alienated.

I worked for the government. I was very hard working, and as a result I got a full scholarship to pursue my masters in agricultural economics in the US. This was not the field of study I wanted to pursue; in fact, I wanted to do an MBA but was told that it was not a development-oriented field of study. So, I figured anything to get out of Lesotho and get back to the US was not a bad idea. I psyched myself to study agricultural economics and figured that I would deal with it. More importantly, I would return to familiar turf. I had enjoyed my time over there and I was going back to be with good friends with whom I had spent memorable times, and that meant a lot to me.

I landed in Illinois, and this time my girlfriend was not around, so I had to adjust to life alone. I decided that this time I had to approach the boyfriend issue differently. I was twenty-four years old, and surely, this was a good time to get involved. But I had no luck at all because I got involved in relationships all for the wrong reasons. I did not know who I was and what I wanted in a relationship. It was basically just the need to conform to standards and to be like everyone else around me. I had never known the difference between love and sex, and I thought that when I loved someone or someone loved me, sex was part of the deal. Well, I was miserable in all those relationships, and guess what? Nothing came out of them. I had a boyfriend from South America whom I really loved and he loved me too, but he told me that when I returned to Lesotho he was sure that the relationship would collapse. I asked him why. He told me that the way I spoke with such negative overtones that I would will it to be over, and, sure enough, that was the end of it when I went back home.

I successfully completed my masters and also got a diploma in cosmetology. Again, with the latter, I thought that I would learn a few tricks on how to look good, because I still believed that I was not attractive. My body was shapely since I had continued with the running, but my face, I believed, still needed a lot of work. I wasn't too thrilled about the masters' qualification I had attained, because this had never been what I wanted to do, but I had done very well and could look forward to the prospect of a job waiting for me.

I returned to Lesotho, once again heartbroken about the relationships that never worked but still hoping that the relationship with my South American would, by some miracle, continue. Well, that never happened, but what did happen was that I resumed communication with the guy I had dated while I was at Duquesne University. He called four times a week, and I felt really loved. I then went to the US for a holiday to visit him a year and half later, and this time around it seemed as if we were headed down the aisle with wedding bells in tow. The family was really happy because they all liked him, and so I started to dream of going to stay in the US on a permanent basis and of the children we would have. My imagination went wild, and I thought that this time God was about to do something great. I was a churchgoer; I went because it was expected but had no relationship with God. At this time, my brother was thinking of getting married soon to his long-time sweetheart, so that was really good for him. I was elated at the prospect of two weddings in the family soon.

On the job front, after getting my masters, I went back to the Ministry of Agriculture. I felt underworked and did not feel challenged at all, so I started prospecting for another job. After my holiday in the US, I got another job, and even though it took me some time to adjust, I liked it. I was challenged and was enjoying doing research in agricultural marketing issues. I had a really good mentor, and now when I look at how far I have come with research skills and writing, I give her the credit. She was so patient and willing to share her years of experience.

By this time, I had a new bunch of friends, and luckily, a primary school friend had come back from the United Kingdom, so we started rebuilding the friendship. She was a Christian and told me that she was now born-again. She told me about salvation, how I needed to repent and to receive Jesus as my Savior. Now, that was not of any interest to me because I was still communicating with my boyfriend in the States, and he was coming to visit Lesotho. And it seemed that with this Jesus in my life I had to live like saint. I figured, let's get married first, since my boyfriend was coming, and we could get engaged, and then the Jesus issue could be revisited. But guess what? My boyfriend never came, and, in fact, the communication soon whittled to nothing. He told me he felt too pressured. He was not ready for marriage, and that broke my heart because I felt so rejected.

I was devastated, and I think that this was the first time that suicide crossed my mind. I started to feel the helplessness and hopelessness of living. What was life all about? How come nothing good had come out of my life? I would cry myself to sleep and wonder why should I go on. Was it worth it? I felt so tired. It was as if I had been on a very long journey but had not got what I had set out to get. Luckily, I did not have to deal with the man who had abused me. I heard that he had left Lesotho soon after we left to go to Rome, and where he was I did not know. Still, I had not disclosed the experience of sexual abuse to anyone. I stayed at home under the protection of my parents. There were nights when I retired to my bedroom early to be on my own. I tried to read the Psalms in the Bible but did not understand them so I would listen to music like Luther Vandross and others and end up feeling worse off.

I felt so alone and I wondered if anyone other than my parents would ever love me. Would I ever experience love? I had traveled the world, the US, Canada, the Bahamas, and Europe, had a good upbringing, attended one of the best universities in the States, had a job, and had purchased my own car, but why was I so sad? Could life get better? I think one of the things that kept me sane was the running. I switched off men from my life and figured that I would never allow myself to be hurt again. Anyone who showed any signs of interest I rejected.

My girlfriend came to me with the Jesus story once again. This time I listened, went to a Pentecostal church with her, and was excited about the message because it touched me. It was very practical, unlike the usual Roman Catholic services I attended. Since nothing had worked for me and I was so miserable, maybe this Jesus story would be the answer. I decided to give it a try since I would not lose anything, and maybe it would get me out of this misery.

At my request, one of the rooms at home was converted into a salon, so during the weekends I was busy doing people's hair. I would relax, braid, and do curly perms; after all, I had the qualifications, and I felt quite proud of myself. I was busy seven days a week and that gave me very little time to reflect on my life. I guess I did not want to deal with it anyway.

Once my friend saw my interest in salvation, she seized the moment and felt encouraged to invite me to church again. I told her that I was busy and that I would come again. For two Sundays, I toyed with the idea, then went back to the Roman Catholic Church. But there was something different about it, and the preaching was not a message of "life." During the next week, I told my friend that I would be in church on Sunday and she did not need to fetch me.

Again, I was touched by the message. I don't remember the exact day, but during the month of May 1993, in my bedroom, I called out to the Lord, said the sinner's prayer, and turned to the Lord. I gave up doing hair on Sunday mornings but still did it on Sunday afternoons. Five years ago, I completely gave up doing hair. It was hard work, and I really did not need the income.

I got involved in the activities of the church, and my life was totally focused on that. I was determined to get a strong foundation for my newly found Christian faith, and luckily, the church I attended welcomed my enthusiasm. My process of maturity was very rapid but came at a great cost. I gave up many friends on the basis that we had nothing in common. It was only much later that I realized that I had developed an attitude, as I immersed myself into church activities, that I was holier than others. I was at church seven days a week and really thought I was headed straight to heaven. Because I was busy with the things of the Lord, I guess I thought it was a good way of escapism. After a while, I felt burdened with this salvation because I was trying too hard to be a good Christian. I began to wonder because we had been taught that freedom came with salvation, and yet I was feeling so bound and not liberated at all. I realized that I was trying in my own power to be a good Christian, but that would not work. I always ended up feeling that I had failed. I learned that it was only by submitting to the Lord that He could change and mould me.

Soon after my salvation (I can't tell the exact date), I had a vision of myself standing before a group of young women. It was as if I was teaching them. When I asked the Lord what this vision meant, I got the sense that I would one day stand before a crowd of young women, but what I would be sharing with them, I did not know. The vision remained at the back of my mind.

As for my ex-boyfriend in the US, he was truly an ex. He had come to Lesotho to visit two years earlier, and when we met, there was nothing between us anymore. I got the impression that he thought that we could catch up and continue just like the good old days, but I was no longer there. I had laid my past aside, at least when it came to him. When I met up with him, I knew that it was the last time. I put closure to that chapter in my life. It was not easy, because I kept thinking "better the devil I know than the one I do not know." I decided to go ahead with my life, and he was not a part of it. When I visited the US again, I never contacted him.

I visited my brother and his family and my friends in the US, and it was wonderful. I spent quality time with his family and my friends. I had a really good time watching the Trinity Broadcasting Network and growing in my Christianity. Since my brother and sister-in-law were both working, I could afford to spend my days as I desired. Both my brother and sister-in-law had recently turned to the Lord, so we had a lot in common. It was good to have fellowship with them, but I realized that I should not be pushy, because salvation is indeed a gift that we receive by God's grace, and we should never boast or think that we are better than others as a result of it. I learned that it is the Lord that saves and that it is not me. I should just be who I am. I must be real. I realized that I had taken my salvation to the extreme and that I needed to have a balanced relationship with the Lord. Going to the States was like going home for me and always a refreshing experience.

I returned to Lesotho invigorated and blessed after having had a good time with old friends, who by now had got married and even had children. It seemed like everyone around me was progressing, but I was caught in a rut. Again, I would say to the Lord, "When does my turn come?"

IV

After the four years I worked at the Research Institute, I decided to fulfill my dream and get an MBA. I had saved sufficient resources and I could finance my studies. I applied to University of Cape Town and needed to do the General Requirement Examinations (GREs). I tried those exams three times and failed to get the required score, so the university did not accept me. I wondered now what the next step would be. A Ph.D. in agricultural economics was not appealing, so I figured I would not do anything but rather continue doing research, which I did. I decided to give up on studies altogether; there had just been too many disappointments, and I did not think that I could deal with any more failures. It was too difficult.

However, through attending one of those GRE sessions, I re-established ties with an old school friend, and I had opportunity to present motivational talks at seminars and conferences that she organized. A precious friendship evolved, which I cherish to this day, so that is one good thing that came out of the failed attempts at the GREs. I figured something good could come out of a seemingly bad situation.

However, another blow was in the offing. My contract terminated at the Institute and there was no hope of renewal. I was out of a job and that was another disappointment. I was substituting for a colleague, so when he came back from further studies, my services were no longer needed. I was informed that there were too many agricultural economists for such a small institute. So, I left and went to sit at home because there was no other job lined up. I thought my world was caving in, and I did not understand why I had to go through so much pain. It was rejection all over again and my low self-esteem was getting lower.

It was at this time that my Christian friend was a pillar of strength for me. She encouraged me and supported me. Together, as we prayed, I asked the Lord to help me not to become bitter toward those who had not renewed the contract. I was unemployed for six months and took the opportunity to go on vacation with my parents to Zimbabwe. It was a good holiday. Even though I was a Christian, I did not understand how this Lord operated, but I tried to look at the bigger picture. Maybe He had something bigger and better in store for me. But, I was not sure and would sometimes have serious doubts.

After the holiday in Zimbabwe, I was then approached to do a consultancy, and I agreed since I was not doing anything and

I needed the cash. I signed the necessary forms, submitted my CV (résumé), and then started work. I guess that because my CV was circulating the offices, I was requested to apply for a one-year post. I thought, why not? The only sad thing was that the salary being offered was lower than what I had been earning, but there did not seem to be another job opportunity on the horizon, so I thought that maybe this was answered prayer, minus the lower salary. As time went on, I found that even though the job was giving me much exposure, it was quite tedious.

To couple this, my boss started to make passes at me, and I knew that I was not going to last in the job. I did not have the energy to deal with sexual harassment, and you would have thought that sexual abuse was enough for a young girl to experience! It was highly stressful and I did not know how to handle it. I resisted his advances, ceased to respect him, and, one day, I threatened him that I would have to report him to higher authorities. He told me that it was just the two of us in his office, so who would believe me? However, after that the advances lessened, but I knew that if he did not go I was going to go. Luckily, he left, but still deep within me, I knew that the job was temporary. Through this experience, I learned that when you are a victim of abuse, you are a "nice" girl, and many times, you get into situations where you are vulnerable to sexual harassment and abuse. You feel guilty saying *no* and allow men to overstep the boundaries.

The Christmas holidays loomed, and December 1997 became a very significant month and year for me. Nineteen years had passed since the sexual abuse, and finally it was time to deal with it. While attending a Christian youth camp in South Africa, I talked to a woman who had in passing mentioned that the church needed to start ministering to those who had been raped, sexually abused, and had AIDS. Suddenly, my experience of sexual abuse hit me very hard. As we traveled back to Lesotho, I cried and cried as I recalled what had happened to me. Luckily, it was dark in the vehicle so these were silent tears I shed and no one knew. I got home subdued and forlorn and the following day went to the computer and wrote and wrote about what I had gone through, but I did not go into detail. I was not ready for that as yet. This was the first step to finally dealing with my past, and it was a great relief.

After writing for about a week, I prayed that the Lord would help me because it was such a painful process. I then printed three copies and gave one to my parents, one to my pastor, and one to my friend. They read them and indeed it was not easy for any of them. I just wanted them all to know who I really was because I felt I had been living a hidden life. It pained me so much when people mentioned that they didn't know why I had become a born-again Christian, because there had been no suffering in my life. They assumed and confidently stated that I had been born with a "silver spoon" and had the best life. So, one lesson is that you should never judge a book by the cover because you don't know what a person has gone through.

Let me start with Mom's reaction. She was so pained and wondered why I had not told her all these years. Dad, too, was really upset and immediately wanted to see if he could trace the perpetrator so that he could kill him. Tears were shed by both of them, and they asked each other many questions because they felt that they had failed as parents in that they had never seen anything. I told them that I did not blame them but felt that it was important for them to know. I guess they felt very helpless and probably blamed themselves, so the issue was not referred to for a while.

My pastor was very sad for me, and she counseled me and told me that I should put it behind me. My friend was speechless and did not know what to say because she had never imagined it. So, I moved on and I continued writing in my journal, and it gave me solace to just get it off my chest. I felt that since there was no one who was able to talk to me at least I could write letters to the Lord and ask questions and tell Him exactly how I felt. He would not judge me, but rather He would love me as I was. I then began to look at the bigger picture, that all this happened for a reason so that I could comfort those who had gone through similar experiences and feared to address the issue. That way, I felt what I had gone through was not in vain.

However, as time went on, I realized that just laying it aside was not the way. I had to deal with the emotions, the reasons for certain behaviors, and everything associated with it before I could proceed with my life. In a way, I felt cheated that those I had confided in had not encouraged me to face and work through my past. But on the other hand, I did not blame them, because they could not begin to imagine the trauma of being sexually abused.

I broached the issue of the abuse to Mom, and she said, "Again, I thought that you had dealt with it." I told her that I needed someone, not to give me advice per se but just someone to listen and asked her if she would be willing to do that. She agreed, and I could see that it was going to be difficult for her, but at least she was also a Christian, so when it became tough, she could pray. I feared to get Dad involved because it had been very difficult for him to accept. There were days when I'd remember something and verbally articulate it to Mom and she would be there for me.

Slowly, slowly, I started to come to terms with the painful past and realized that certain actions were a result of what I had gone through. These actions included staying at home with my parents for the longest time, unlike my siblings who had long left the nest, because I was afraid to be on my own, and the fact that I never stayed in the States like my brother did after graduating, because I did not want to be on my own; I wanted the security of being at home. I did not like taking risks. I always wanted to do things with predictable outcomes. There would be too much uncertainty involved with living in the US. I wanted routine and not the unexpected.

However, I did not make time to deal with my past because I had a full life. I was active in church activities. I was now making time to spend with non-Christian friends, and I had joined the

Toastmasters Club. I was not involved in any relationship, and I think that was because I feared to get involved. I did not know what a relationship was all about, and it seemed that sex was always the ultimate; whether it took a week or a month to get there, it was always looming on the horizon. So, I just became unapproachable, and, interestingly, many times, it was married men who made advances at me. This used to bother me, and I wondered if they saw that I had had sex with men of their type.

I remember one time I met a man. He was so good looking and irresistible, so when he asked me out, I immediately agreed to meet him. He did have a gold wedding band on the fourth finger of the left hand, but that was conveniently overlooked. Later, when I realized the mistake I had made, I told my Christian friend about the date, and she later came up with a plan. The plan was that we would meet with him and then tell him that we were going to a friend's. He was one of those types of men, living life in the fast lane. Little did he know that we would take him to our pastor's home. Well, when we got there and had settled down, our pastor introduced himself and his family, and you should have seen the look on his face. That afternoon must have been a serious ordeal for him, but he had no choice and had to sit through it because we had gone in my car. Well, after we dropped him off, we knew that we would not see or hear from him again, and that is exactly what happened. We also hoped that he had learned a lesson not to make passes at single girls. My friend was truly a godsend because I did not know how to deal with that situation.

Relationships with men were one of the greatest struggles I had to deal with. After the above experience, you would think that would be the last time I would get into such situations, but it was not. Even though I despised married men, I did not know how to behave toward them. I knew that not all of them had sexually abused me, so I could at least talk to them. I was nice and not assertive, so my "No" was many times interpreted as "Yes." I thought that there was nothing wrong with being nice to them, and it was clear in my mind that I would not have a sexual relationship with them.

However, this got me into trouble on numerous occasions, until I learned that it's not possible to have a platonic relationship with a married man. Mom always warned me that a married man is trouble, especially when he wants to get too close, and she shared stories of her youthful days when she would often flee from them because they were not looking for a wife in her but ultimately for sex.

I thought she was wrong, but I have since learned that in the back of many married men's minds is sex. It is not marriage they are looking for, so it is just for fun, and that means sex. I may seem to be unfair, but my experience has shown that. I learned much later to avoid entertaining any close relationship with them, and at least I have become assertive, and my no is an emphatic no, which does not leave a shadow of doubt that I mean yes.

In looking for ways not to attract men, I picked up a habit of looking straight through them. I do not allow my eyes to meet with them and basically do not see them. This I adopted to protect myself from them, and it made me very unapproachable. I guess I was putting up walls.

One thing I used to hate about some of the men I came into contact with is that they would ask me when I was going to invite them for lunch or cook for them. I'd wonder why they didn't ask me for a date and why did they want to come to my house. I'd conclude that it was because they wanted sex. Maybe I was incorrect, but with a past of sexual abuse, it's a logical deduction. In my mind, I wanted a man who would just be a friend and would not impose issues of sex upon me. When I shared my dream with my friends, they wondered which planet I came from and figured that I was asking for the impossible, because in this day and age very few men just wanted to be friends. However, I still clung to my dream.

Christian single men that I knew were very few, so that limited my choices of finding a prospective mate. However, I was very adamant that I had to be yoked with a believer because he would understand my stance of no sex before marriage. My Christian girlfriend and I made marriage partners a feature on our prayer list and decided to go on ahead with other more constructive activities. I did have a good non-Christian male friend, and we would sometimes do things together, but I never perceived him as anything more than a friend. Dad and others did not understand what the big deal was, because this friend of mine, as a result of hanging around me, would ultimately become a Christian.

However, I was adamant that any man I dated had to be a Christian prior to my involvement with him. But to be honest, there were many times when my friend and I got impatient and thought that maybe we could start looking for those who could be converted. But then our pastor would preach on a Sunday morning about the benefits of waiting upon the Lord for a partner. That would dash our hopes and we would lay our ideas aside. So, we put the marriage issue aside and decided that it was better that the Lord deal with it in His time.

But it was not easy, because time and time again people would prophesy that they saw me getting married, etc., but none of it came to pass. That desire to be married would surface again, but my reasons were not valid because, mind you, I was not even sure if I could relate with the male species. But still, I wanted to get married. Well, the years passed by, and I began to wonder whether I would ever get married and started thinking that maybe after what had happened to me no one would want me. Maybe I was not good enough for anyone, because friends all around me were getting married, and there was no one in the picture for me. I felt waves of rejection and the unfairness of life.

My friends would ask me to be maid of honor or a bridesmaid at their weddings, and I wondered when my time would come. In Lesotho, there is this belief that if you are a maid of honor on several occasions, you will not get married. So, Mom began to raise this issue. I thought that maybe I was cursed. I really had to pray that the Lord would help me not to become bitter and jealous of my friends but rather to rejoice with them. So, I made a choice to be truly happy for them and believed that my time would come. Maybe God was not finished with me yet. I realized that maybe He had to help me to really work on my past and all the damage that had happened, and then maybe things would change.

V

In the meantime, work was coming on slowly, and I was not content with the uncertainty of my contract being renewed on a yearly basis, so I felt that it was time to start prospecting for another job. I wanted to leave Lesotho but not to go to South Africa. I wanted to go to a country where there were no Basotho people I knew, but I did not know where. So, we prayed, because my Christian friend was also looking for a job elsewhere. By this time, I had moved out of my parent's house. I was now living on my own and kept busy most of the time. It was sad to leave home, but I knew that it was time to leave the sheltered environment. I had to now go and face life on my own. Mom felt hesitant and wondered whether I would cope, but she was comfortable since I was just four kilometers away from home.

I moved into a two-bedroom flat, furnished it, and lived very comfortably. Only close female friends had access into my home.

No males, because, again, I did not want my privacy to be invaded. At the back of my mind, there was a feeling that if I liked a man, would I have enough courage and strength to resist him? By now, I realized that no matter how strong your relationship is with the Lord, it's not easy to resist temptation, so better to avoid it. As a result, men were not welcome guests. It's amazing how once something is taught to you at a young age, it remains engraved in your mind. My folks taught us that decent girls do not invite men to their house, so even to this day men do not just walk into my home.

I had been in Lesotho for eight years since returning from the US and felt that I had given it my best shot. I had worked in government, at the university, and for an international agency, so where else could I go? I felt crowded in Maseru and needed a bigger place so that I could grow as an individual. The idea of going back to the US was appealing, and I knew one of the easiest ways would be to go pursue my doctorate. But knowing that I had not particularly enjoyed the agricultural economics program, the idea of spending four years doing a program I did not enjoy did not sound appealing.

The prospect of living in the US was not an option, and I figured that I would have to be content with just visits. I had tossed out the window the prospect of getting an MBA and figured that was not the Lord's plan for me. Again, I thought that as far as career went, the Lord had forsaken me, because, in that field, nothing was working out. I decided to forget about studies and rather see how I could get out of Lesotho.

I felt sad for my folks while I was planning to leave Lesotho because it would leave just the two of them. My sister was settled in Zimbabwe with her three children, and my brother was settled in the US with his wife and one child. How I envied my brother for taking the risk of staying in the US after he graduated. I admired him because he was happily married and successful. I wondered what would have become of me if I had stayed in the US. As for my ex-boyfriend in the US, I had no regrets about not marrying him, because I felt that the marriage would not have lasted. We both had too many unresolved issues.

I knew that if I stayed in Lesotho, I would one day have regrets about not taking a journey to an unknown place. I did not want to live a life of blaming my parents for holding me back from living my life. It must have been very hard for both of them, but I felt it more for my father. He had worked so hard to achieve all that he had attained, and there was none of us to manage or to appreciate the family property. It was as if all his efforts were in vain, but I hoped that he would understand that he had given us exposure to, or a taste of, something else when we left for Italy ten years ago. I hoped that he would truly release us and go on with his life without having any bitterness.

Then in the *Mail & Guardian,* a South African newspaper, my Christian friend spotted an advertisement inviting applications for a researcher post in an economic unit in Namibia, and the qualifications sought were what I had. She encouraged me to apply, but I did not. However, she did not let me get off easily and kept pressing me until I finally applied. I was short-listed and got called in for an interview, which I passed, and an offer was proposed.

I knew the Lord's hand was in this, and I felt like Abram in the Bible, whom the Lord told to leave his country, his people, his father's household, and to go to the land He would show him. So, I resigned from my previous job, and, with great trepidation and fear, I knew this was it. I was fully convinced that I was going to deal with my past once and for all so that I could move on with my life and be what God had intended. I packed my belongings and tried to sell my car, but no one wanted to purchase it for a reasonable price. So, I drove out to Windhoek with Mom. She also knew that it was final and felt that for the year that I had been staying alone the Lord had been preparing them for my imminent departure.

Well, I settled into my job and soon found a place to stay. Because I did not know anyone in Windhoek, I now had to deal with myself and started on a long journey of accepting, forgiving, and loving myself. The holidays were tough, because I went to the shops and returned home without talking to anyone. Then it was back to spending time with the Lord. I did watch some television, but I am not a fan of it, so it would be music and quiet time for me. A song that encouraged me was "He's Always There" by Cece Winans. It reminded me that no matter where I go,

He is always with me, and that gave me the courage to keep on with the journey. I wrote in my journal, asked questions, and cried for my lost virginity at such a young age, for the lost years when I could not be myself, for being forced to mature so quickly, and for being so lonely. I refrained from calling home often because I wanted to grow up and get on with my life.

I had questions for the Lord, such as why He had allowed this to happen. Then I remembered that He had already told me the reason. One issue I struggled with was trusting the Lord. I only trusted Him to a certain extent, after which I would take over. I had learned to become independent, and I felt that with certain things I did not need God. After all, when I needed Him most, He was nowhere to be found. I had never before had a time like this when I could confront so many issues that had not been addressed. It was a painful but inevitable process.

I learned to appreciate my own company and started to discover my talents, such as writing, which had been buried. When God wants to deal with you, there is no running away, and this was the time for me. I also realized that I did not love myself; in fact, I despised myself. Looking in the mirror at myself naked was a no-no. I had to force myself to look at myself and to appreciate the way that the Lord wonderfully formed me. This process of digging and searching took all the time I was in Namibia because it is not an overnight process.

I started scouting around for a place to worship on Sundays and visited a number of places. I settled with one church because

I felt I was welcome. I am thankful for the pastor, who saw the leadership skills in me, and soon I became a leader in the church. It was something natural and not new, because in Lesotho, I had been a youth leader. I met wonderful people at church and made some great and very special friendships. These folks embraced me and took me in as part of their families to the extent that I knew I was not alone in Windhoek. It was a beautiful experience. The Lord sent my way one woman who was so special. From the minute we met, we connected. It is amazing how the friendship evolved. She embraced me and showered me with love to the extent that I knew I could rely on her and that she would do anything for me. This was truly a godsend, and through her friendship I learned that friendship is a precious gift, which I was blessed to have received.

For the very first time in my life, I could be me without any pretensions. I could share my experiences and be totally real. Living a life of pretensions became a thing of the past. Accepting compliments was something I had to consciously work on, and when people gave me compliments I had to receive them. I was always good at giving compliments and making people feel special, but I felt that I was not worthy to receive them because I was not special. I knew that the Word of God says we are special, but I had to internalize it, which took time.

My vision started to become more concrete, and I knew I would be working with young girls and women who were hurting and wounded, to comfort them and encourage them that there is hope. My own life is a testimony of that. I did not know where and when that vision would happen, but it was in me, and I shared it with my pastor. I also made a decision to share my past abuse with other people because I strongly believe that is one way people can open up and start to share. I saw from my own experience that sexual abuse is not an issue that is openly discussed, but in order for victims like me to get healed, we need to start talking. It was a small step, but at least it was a start, which I was committed to pursue.

I did meet some interesting men, but by this time, I had matured, so I knew that non-Christian men would not be in the cards. I must admit that having a boyfriend who was not a Christian did cross my mind, but when I thought of the couples I knew of whom one spouse was a Christian and the other one was not, I decided to wait upon the Lord for a man who had a personal relationship with the Lord. Sometimes I wonder whether that is not a way to avoid getting involved with a man. However, meeting Christian single men proved to be a very difficult challenge in Windhoek. But there was one whom I met unexpectedly, who is worthy of mention, and as the friendship evolved, I really liked him. However, nothing was to come out of that relationship. Just as unexpectedly as it had started, it unexpectedly ended. I did battle trying to forget him, thinking that it was me who was the problem and maybe I was putting pressure on him. However, over time, I told myself that I was not to blame and that some things are just not meant to be.

Interestingly, the issue of a man in my life was really not an issue because I was too busy and most of the time too exhausted to dwell on that. I was content that being busy meant that I was involved in constructive activities. I put the men issue aside and maybe gave up on the idea of meeting an eligible man in Windhoek. There just did not seem to be any eligible Christian men, so I ceased to have any expectations.

I had met a man in Lesotho and got to know him casually but when I got to Namibia, we forged a very good friendship. He was a married man, and, of course, not eligible, but a good friend. We did not meet often because he was not a resident in Windhoek, but when we met we engaged in discussions ranging from development and social problems, spirituality, human relationships, and life in general. The friendship was platonic, and there was mutual respect, so through this friendship, I learned that there are some married men with whom one can have a platonic friendship, but it is not the norm.

I do not despise married men and have since forgiven the man who sexually abused me. I know that I will not get sexually involved with a married man or a single man out of wedlock. I know that once you get sexually involved a bond develops, and it's difficult to disentangle yourself from it. From a woman's perspective, when you lose your virginity you give of yourself and your innermost being, and if it is not reciprocal, you can be scarred for life.

Once again, one-and-a-half years after getting to Namibia, I felt the urge to go to the US and planned a six-week visit. I decided that I would visit my brother and his family and my friends and examine the prospect of pursuing graduate studies. The Ph.D. issue lurked in my mind again and seemed like the right thing to do given that I was working in a research/consultancy institute. That dream of going to live in the US had not disappeared and was still alive in me. I somehow seemed to have reached a dead end with my career plans, but I thought that I would benefit professionally by pursuing my Ph.D. After all, I had been out of university for ten years and thought that this might be the right time to consider graduate studies. I had worked on a number of issues in my life and felt that I was ready for studies.

I headed to the US and started off in New Jersey. Then I went to Waynesboro in Pennsylvania, then to Washington DC, and finally to Los Angeles. When I landed in New York, it was again like I had come home. It was familiar turf and good to see the welcoming faces of beloved friends and family. I had a really good time in the US and spent Christmas with my brother and his family. I really missed my brother. Not having seen him for four years was not easy, but we had learned to live with it. We talked about our childhood days, our parents, our sister, and our lives as Christians. It was wonderful, and when time came to say goodbye, it was difficult. We hoped for a time when I could live closer to him and his family. Luckily, I have a beautiful relationship with my sister-in-law and I respect her. She is a good woman and wife for my brother. Despite his making fun of my legs, we've had a good relationship that has developed over the years. Many times he forgets and thinks I am his younger sister, so he can be quite protective, which is special. Sadly, just when I was bonding with my niece and nephew, I had to leave, and we have to rely on the telephone and emails to keep in touch.

I had a lot of time to muse over issues while I was in the US and that was namely my singleness, which was highlighted on Christmas day. As my brother and his family were opening gifts and enjoying the family unity, I felt alone. They never made me feel excluded, but it hit me that I do not have any family and, in actual fact, I am alone. No spouse and no children, so it was rather depressing, but I decided to quickly get out of that mode. I accepted the status quo knowing that it would not change immediately, but rather, I should make the most of the holidays.

The marriage issue kept lurking again, and I wondered and asked the Lord when my status would change. Surely, we had been working on the whole issue of my past and was it not yet time? Silence was my answer, and I again laid the issue aside. After all, I was headed back to Namibia soon and there was no prospect in sight, so better I forget the issue. However, I figured that maybe if I should get to graduate school I might have a wider circle of people to meet and might possibly meet "that" man. This gave me increased motivation to apply to a number of schools.

I returned to Namibia feeling refreshed and highly motivated because in my mind I reckoned my time in Namibia was short and I was headed for some exciting opportunities. I applied to different schools and, believe me, when responses started flowing back, none of the universities I had applied to accepted me. I was so disappointed and disillusioned. While I was getting responses, the thought, what I would do if none of the universities accepted me, crossed my mind.

I started to ask the Lord what more I had to do here and told Him that He would have to guide me because now I had seen my plans all fall to naught. Through this experience I learned a lesson, which was that it is better to put everything into God's hand and to surrender to His will because it is the safest place in the world. I had to learn to relinquish my plans to Him, which meant entrusting my life to Him. I still had not learned to do this, but this time I had no choice and gave over everything to Him and told Him that it would be His will not mine. Career plans, marriages, further studies, and all. I figured I had better give them to the Lord, because whatever I tried to follow up on seemed to fail.

So having failed to gain admission into a Ph.D. program, I asked the Lord what was my career path to be, because I was not quite sure about the field of agricultural economics. I found it to be too abstract, clinical, and with no human element to it. I guess that is why I turned to HIV/AIDS as the focus of my research, because it gave me the possibility of dealing with human beings.

This was not to say that I did not enjoy my work. To the contrary, I felt privileged to have the opportunity to learn about the Namibian economy and to be exposed to diverse topics of research. However, in performing my duties, I was also questioning myself about my career path.

I realized that this was an issue I had never reflected upon, and as I thought more about it, I figured that my career choices were built upon the life experiences I had gone through. Maybe if I had not been sexually abused I would have made other choices. I settled for whatever came my way, without really looking at the personality traits I had. In fact, I don't ever remember having chosen business administration because I loved it, and as for agricultural economics, I did it because a full scholarship was awarded to me and I thought, why should I not take it?

The desire to study was deep within me, and I felt that the time was right. I toyed with the idea of public health, but it did not seem quite right. Then I asked myself what my extracurricular activities entailed—did I go home and read an agricultural economics or an economics journal? The answer was no, and then I realized that I read a lot of self-help books and spent much time on the telephone, counseling and mentoring. I realized that I loved working with people, and my objective in life was to make a positive difference in other people's lives, no matter how small my effort. So many people just gave me the opportunity to see my other talents and gifts. Someone unexpectedly came into my life and opened another door that afforded me to do what I had been doing in Lesotho and that was delivering motivational talks. This was the beginning of an unexpected friendship that has developed into something "beautiful."

After further reflection and prayers, one Wednesday, when I was in church, counseling/psychology with the University of South Africa (UNISA) came into my heart. I left that meeting rejoicing in my heart and with my heart at total peace. The Lord had answered me, and the next day I checked the website to see how I could enroll in the psychology program. In a way, it was a great relief to have found an area that I could relate to after so many years of not quite knowing which direction to take. It had taken me twelve long years to discover this, and I was very excited.

Finally, the door also opened for me to be involved in mentoring and counseling young girls who were hurting and wounded. I remembered the vision. Eight years had passed, and I realized that the Lord had just given me a glimpse then of what He had in store for me. However, I discovered that I had to be healed before I could work with the young women, and what a fulfilling experience it is to give of myself to the young women. I have so much to be grateful for. I had to leave my native country for the Lord to deal with me, heal me, and set me free to be a blessing to others. I joined up with a pastor from another church to work with the Daughters of Destiny. How the Daughters came into my life is amazing.

In 2001, my pastor nominated me to attend a leadership seminar in Hawaii, and I was ready to back off at the last minute. I had never attended a Christian seminar, so I did not know what to expect. I was not a pastor but just a leader, so I was unsure whether I would fit in. Anyway, my pastor left the decision up to me, and I decided that I would go ahead on this mission because it was not by accident that I had been selected. I was going with another lady, a pastor from another church, and we headed to Maui for a month's seminar. It was an experience I shall never forget.

We learned so much, and in talking, I learned about the Daughters of Destiny from the pastor. The Daughters were a group of young women who were hurting because they had been rejected, sexually abused, or were going through other crises. In ministering to or counseling the young women, the love of Christ was shared. The young women ranged in age from thirteen to twenty-five years. Some of them worked, or studied in university, and others were in school. Not all were Christians. However, we believed that it was through the realization of God's love that they could overcome, so we encouraged them to come to know the Lord. As these young women got healed, they could then have the compassion to love others and minister to them.

What the pastor was doing sounded commendable and honorable, and it was also my calling to minister to hurting young women. I really admired this woman and knew that I would be a part of the Daughters of Destiny. I knew that my prayers had been answered. I was thrilled about this possibility.

The seminar was so intense that I did not have much time to meditate on the issue, but I knew that I had to get more involved in a ministry with hurting and wounded young women. The Lord had laid this burden on my heart so strongly. I met many women from all walks of life and forged some very good friendships. Getting to know such a variety of women from so many countries was a rare opportunity. When I shared my story about sexual abuse with these women, the pastor asked me whether I would share it with the Daughters once we got back to Namibia and I agreed. After the Haggai seminar, we were greatly enriched and filled with a greater purpose to do what we had outlined in our goal-setting sessions. I knew that I could not ever be the same again.

A few months later, the pastor contacted me to share my testimony of sexual abuse with the Daughters, and I had a blessed time with them. I fell in love with the young women, and I was convinced that this was what the Lord had called me to do. However, mentoring these young women was a lot of hard work, and it was very interesting that, in some of their actions and reactions, I could relate with them so well. What I learned while dealing with my experience with sexual abuse and imparting it to the young women was that they had to come to a point in their lives where they wanted to move ahead. No one but they could relive the painful events of the past, but in order for that to happen they needed to forgive themselves and embrace the fact that the Lord loved them.

So, what had my time in Namibia meant for me? It had been a critical milestone, a season for me to uncover my past and rediscover myself before I could step out to the next phase. It had not been an easy journey but I was determined to move forward, I was hungry for change and I was open to new challenges. I had come to realize that so much of my past had influenced who I was. All along, I had dismissed my actions with the hope that the past would disappear like a vapor, but that never happened. The past had been like a shroud upon me and manifested itself in so many of my behaviors and thoughts. I went around carrying all the rubbish inside, thinking that I had progressed in life yet I had remained stagnant—at that place where I had experienced pain and suffering. I was one out of the many women who had buried past hurts and put on all the emotional "makeup." I had devised coping strategies to deal with the pain. Issues had been shelved in the deepest recesses of my subconscious, never to be addressed.

I went about not really knowing where I was headed or what I wanted out of life because I had been so hurt. I hid my pain and suffering very well as I went about my daily business, but deep down I was so fragile and at night, I would drench my pillow with tears. If someone looked closely, they might have detected some sadness or loneliness. I readily accepted anything that looked like love, even from men who were not necessarily good for me. I did not see the warning signs, and even if I did, I ignored them because I wanted so badly to be "normal" (i.e. conforming to the norms of society) like everyone else. I ended up in wrong relationships that didn't last because I had not dealt with the past. I wanted to please everyone because I feared to hurt those around me, even to my own detriment.

Once I embarked on a long journey of self-discovery, first with some trepidation, I worked through so many emotions, such as the fear of not being accepted; regret for the childhood that I had lost prematurely; being betrayed by a family friend; the constant feeling of guilt; the struggle with self-pity and mistrust; the uncertainty of love and most importantly, having to forgive the man who had abused me and also to forgive myself. I do not know where you are in your own journey but maybe, you have also struggled with these emotions and can relate to them. I expressed them as poems and would like to share them with you in the next chapter. As these emotions flowed from deep within me, I was compelled to write them down, and it was a very therapeutic process as I attempted to make sense of what sexual abuse had done to me.

I was at a point where I felt so good about the progress that I had made. I was now able to share my experience with others and to use my testimony as a way for others to see that they were not the only ones who had gone through a traumatic event. The vision that I had soon after I had become a Christian had come to pass and when I worked with young women, I was truly at peace and derived great fulfillment and a sense of purpose. I looked forward to other opportunities to work with young women. I had even learned to give and receive hugs.

I found the courage to pursue a field of study- psychology- and that I would never have imagined before. I had made a choice to forgive the man who had abused me and had accepted the fact that I was a victim. I was now able to assert myself and say no to what I did not want to do without feeling guilty. I still had other issues to work on such as male-female relationships, which were a struggle but given time, I knew that I would deal with them.

CROSSING OVER

You have been hurt.
You have been rejected.
You have been abandoned.
You have been abused.
Your self-esteem and confidence have been
shattered.
You don't love yourself.
You don't believe in yourself.
You don't think that you will amount to anything.

Why continue living?
What is the point?
Getting by from day to day is tough.
And if that's what life is all about, is it worth it?
I have cried and cried.
I have soaked my pillow with tears.
It seems as though there are no more tears left.
But the well of tears continues to overflow.
The crying has not made the situation any better,
but at least I got some relief.
I delve into my work as a distraction
to forget the pain.
I hide it in my subconscious where I don't have
to deal with the pain.
I excel in my work.
Any task given I perform with excellence
to gain commendation.
No one sees the pain I carry.
I put on a façade,
Seemingly giving the impression that all is well.
But behind that mask, a soul is crying,
a soul is in need.
How many of us have masks and behind them
souls are crying out in despair?
Pain hidden so well,
Those very close cannot figure it out.

They wonder why the cold response
when they reach out in love.
They think I am afraid of being touched.
I am.
I once trusted and agreed to be touched,
but I got burned.
They don't know, but if only they knew....
I hide the pain and learn to cope.
I go from day to day.
I put a smile on my face and yet I am hurting.
Relationships are strained
and they never seem to last.
I don't express my feelings; how can I?
I don't know how.
I fear to give to the relationship fully,
and I am in it half-heartedly,
for it is the thing to do.
I don't open up totally and I can't relax.
All too soon, the relationship is over.
I willed it to happen, for I do not expect
any good thing for me.
How?
Me, who is so filthy?
I tell myself that I don't deserve it.
I don't love myself; in fact,
I hate myself.

I don't know who I am.
Then it dawns on me that I cannot go on like this.
Loneliness and emptiness well within me.
Work fails to fill the void.
Everything I try fails to fill the void.
There is something I need, and I can't figure what it is until I meet my Savior.
I cry out to Him and He hears my cry.
He lifts me out of the mud and mire.
He puts my feet on the rock and gives me a firm place to stand.
He puts a new song into my mouth.
I put my all into knowing Him,
Having an intimate relationship with Him.
I call unto Him and burrow deeper to know Him.
This is a better haven,
for He can never abandon me.
I turn away from relationships
with humankind, particularly men.
Then He teaches me that it's not the way
He wants it, for He has called me
to relate with humankind.
He has made all men in His likeness
and image and loves His creation.
So, that is another lesson to learn.
He teaches me to love myself.

He tells me that He has a plan for me.
He whispers words of encouragement.
He gives me reason to live.
He teaches me to hope.
He tells me in more ways than one
that He loves me.
He restores my self-confidence, because,
in His eyes, I am not a mistake.
I begin to love myself.
It is not an overnight process.
I encourage myself through His word.
I see how He sees me—as unique
and beautiful.
And there is no other person like me.
If I do not fulfill what He has called me to do,
it will not be done.
There is a meaning and purpose after all.
I hold my head high.
I walk with confidence because
I know who I am in Christ.
You might call me arrogant or proud,
but you do not know where I have been.
You don't know what it has taken
for me to get here.
It has been a long journey,
but the bottom line is that I have made it.
And at last, I have crossed over from a
meaningless life to one of victory.

BETRAYED

How could he do it?
A father with children,
some were almost my age.
Games we would play together,
either at their house or our house.
Days filled with laughter and fun.
Until that day, I was betrayed....
My laughter and joy died on that day.
He robbed me of my childhood,
and all too soon, I became a woman.
What could I do? Who could I tell?
Who would believe me?
I ceased to trust that day.
I became withdrawn and silenced,
so that I would not give away too much.
Deep within, the pain and grief,
I had to subdue.
Over and over again, I relived that terrible day
and all the other days that followed.
He was obsessed with me and would stalk me;
and then, thank God,
for His faithfulness.
He will not let you be tempted

beyond what you can bear.
He left and we left the country.
But the feelings never leave.
They remained etched,
but I chose to shelve them.
What else could I do at fourteen years old?
I had to go on as if nothing happened,
and that I did....
Till that day, when it was time to dig and dig.
I had to move beyond the fourteen-year-old girl
and confront the emotions,
once and for all.

FEAR

Like the tentacles of an octopus, it grips me,
immobilizes me, and there is no moving forward.
I am caught up in a trap.
Sometimes barely noticing it.
Time passes.
What I could have done is not done.
Then I realize that fear is irrational—False
Evidence Appearing Real.
Fear to move forward stifles me.
Who knows what tomorrow brings?
I get caught up in the past.
I fear to love, fear to let go,
and fear to trust because I have been hurt so bad.
But God calls and says, "It's time to open up,
time to love, time to let go,
and time to trust."
Can I do so?
It's not easy, and a battle rages within me,
and so much turmoil.
It's so much easier to be in the comfort zone.
But that is not living.
Risk is part of living.
To love, to trust, and to let go is a risk.
But God will provide me with all that I need.
It's not easy, but I rely on His faithfulness....

REGRETS

If I could turn the clock back again, I'd reclaim
the childhood that I lost all too soon.
Through no act of mine,
it was taken away from me.
It was stripped as the petals of a rose
that has not yet blossomed.
The rose was not allowed to mature.
I, too, like the rose, was not allowed to develop
into a free-spirited child.
It is interesting how such an act can be a painful
reminder in later years
and how it destroys the life of that adult.
I look at the fourteen-year-old girls around me
and pray that they be allowed to grow
to maturity and their childhood will not
be stripped away.
I cry for others who have gone through
the anguish and pain.
But I know that even in going through that pain,
there is a God who works all things for the good
of those who love Him and have been called
according to His purposes.
He turns evil into good, ugliness into beauty,

negative into positive, and darkness into day.
Even in the midst of all those
turbulent circumstances
God is in control, and He is able
to calm the storms.
The regret will remain in my heart,
but I choose not to dwell on it.
But instead I focus on what He has
planned for me.

GUILT

Washes over me like a river
When any good thing happens to me
I feel that it should not have happened to me
I did not deserve it
I cannot accept it
After what has happened to me
How can it really be true?
Every small thing I do not do
and the guilt glares at me
I get frustrated and spend so much time asking
for God's forgiveness
I don't move forward because
I doubt God's forgiveness
I get caught up in a trap and lose focus
Until I begin to realize that God
is a God of love
That He surely forgives
And that this guilt is unreasonable
I must lay it aside and get on with
more rewarding tasks.

SEEKING FOR APPROVAL

Always pushing myself to the extremes, setting standards that are too high
To prove to myself and to others that I am a success.
Always trying to prove myself, so that I can be acknowledged and loved.
I feel that after what I have been through no one really loves me for who I am.
Over the years, I never disclosed my secret but kept it within me.
I feared that if I spoke no one would approve of me.
Instead, people would condemn me or blame me for what happened.
They would love me less and not understand, so it was better to hide my true identity.
But, oh it was painful not to feel worthy to be loved....
Now, I seek approval not from man but from the Lord and strive to be at peace with myself....
That is sheer bliss and totally liberating!

SELF-PITY

When you have not embarked
on the journey of life,
When confusion rages and you don't know who
you are and where you are going,
When you have not learned to be content with
who you are Pity parties are the norm,
rather than the exception.
Let me tell you about pity parties....
I am sure that you have been to one of them.
I have been to several of them.
And much as the experience
is not altogether exciting,
There were those days when I couldn't
seem to avoid them.
It would start with a small thought,
Feeling unloved or wondering where the Lord
was in the midst of all my suffering.
Before I knew it,
I started feeling pity for myself.
Suddenly, there was a host of guests
at the party,
Discouragement, Bitterness,
Anger, Loneliness, and others

Who were out to have the party
of their lives at my expense.
After all, I had invited them,
because when you invite one,
The others also come,
even if they are uninvited.
At this point, I did not know how
 to chase them away,
So they would stay a couple of days,
Influencing my thoughts and behaviors.
I would accommodate them
and justify their presence
On the grounds that it was normal
for me to be down and depressed.
But, I have come a long way and learned that it is
not a good idea to entertain pity parties.
They are a waste of time....
So when thoughts come,
which often they do,
And are leading me to a pity party,
I reject the thoughts and replace them
with pleasant ones,
Because that is one route I refuse to go.
Pity parties are events of the past.
I have been to too many of them, and no more
feeling sorry for myself....

LETTING GO

Letting go.
Sounds so easy but yet so hard.
Seems so much easier to hold onto what I know,
what I am sure of....
Rather than let go.
To walk into what I do not know,
what I am uncertain about.
The unknown, the deep waters...
What an illusion, what a lie...
I realize that I need to let go.
Time is passing.
Every minute and every second counts as I hold
tightly onto the reins of the past.
I refuse to let God take over.
I prevent my blessings from spilling over, and the
bottom line is that I have been hurt.
Where was God in the midst of it all?
I do not trust God.
But now, I see the need to let go.
I ask, "How can I let go?"
I don't know how, and He whispers to me, "I'll
show you how! Let go off the reins to Me. Let Me
be God. Trust Me, just try and believe Me, for

those who trust in Me shall never be put to
shame. That is My word, and My beloved child,
I honor My word
more than anything."
I respond, "Oh, Lord, I'd love to give You the
reins, but how do I do it practically?"
He says I should lift my eyes heaven-bound and
say, "In the name of Jesus Christ of Nazareth,
I choose to let go to you, dear God!"
I say, "Take control, lead me, and guide me.
If I falter and take the reins from You, remind me
of what I chose to do. Take the reins from me,
and You take me where You want me to go.
Where You have always wanted me to go,
because I choose to hold on."
I take my first steps.
Every day gets better,
as I have chosen to let go.
Learning to trust in God.
Truly leaning on Him,
instead of on me.
What a challenge....
But with Him,
I'll not go astray.
I know I'll overcome
and see the goodness of the Lord.

FORGIVENESS

Is not an easy thing
One holds on to the pain and hurt
Wishing to never see that person again
Wishing that the person who hurt you could die.
I was so numb
I blocked him out
I refused to remember how he looked
But in order to move forward
I brought back images of him, painful as it was,
so that I could forgive
I knew that if I did not forgive,
he would have a hold on me
Bitterness and anger would surface in me
I had seen many women who were so bitter
because of a man
I decided that I was not going to be
like one of them.
Since I was never meant to meet him,
and to this day, I do not know where he is
I decided that I would close that chapter
of my life, once and for all
I called out his name and uttered words
of forgiveness aloud

On the grounds that the Lord forgave me of every one of my sins and who was I to refuse to forgive
I was set free
When thoughts of him would surface, I would have compassion on this man.
You see forgiveness is a choice that you make
It requires you to look beyond yourself and to humble yourself
And it means that you also have to forgive yourself of the acts that you committed against yourself
At that time, you acted as well as you could given the information or knowledge that you had
It's time to stop being so hard on yourself and rather embrace forgiveness as your friend.

LOVE

Never understood what love was.
My understanding of it was totally distorted; I would ask myself, *Is sex love or is love sex?*
I couldn't understand what love was for the longest time.
It was a concept I could not deal with, for there was so much conflict in my mind associated with it.
The man who abused me said that he loved me, but at the same time he did things to me that hurt me....
I was not able to handle a situation when someone declared love for me, particularly a man.
I still have a problem when someone says that he loves me.
I get flustered and anxious because I ask myself if that person does not just want sex.
I feel that once a person says he loves me I have to give something in return, and that something is sex.
I have recently understood what love is all about.
I always heard that Jesus loves me, but I did not believe it.

It was a challenge to believe it, but one day, I accepted that Jesus loves me unconditionally.
I realized that I did not have to give Him anything, but all He wanted was for me to embrace His love freely.
Despite who I am and what I have done,
He loves me just as I am.
I am comforted by the love of Jesus, so all I do is accept it, regardless of how I feel.
And then a man came into my life.
He told me that he loved me.
At first, I did not believe him and wondered what he wanted.
I suspected it was sex and told myself that time would tell.
I went through so many emotions and did not want to believe him; but over time, he persevered and kept on telling me that he loved me.
Actions speak louder than words, and with his actions he proved that he loved me.
He tirelessly gave of himself to me and always ensured that I was at ease and comfortable.
He didn't ask for anything in return.
He didn't impose himself or his desires upon me,
He respected me, and he was patient with me.
If I doubted his love for me, I have been shown otherwise.

I asked the Lord why He brought him my way,
and I am convinced that it is because He wanted
me to see that love is possible and that a man can
be trusted.
I know that this was an important part of the
healing process.
For this, I am thankful.
It was a friendship that came about for a reason
and a season,
And now, that season is over,
so it is time to move on....

A VALLEY EXPERIENCE

The valleys are an essential element of life.
Imagine if life were just mountaintops?
We would never grow, because, in order for us to
go from one glory to another, we need the valleys
of life.
The valleys toughen and strengthen us.
While we are in the valley, we think that we are
the only ones in the valley.
We don't realize that some valleys are deeper than
others and that the one you are in,
you can get out of it.
It's painful while you are in it, and you wonder
why the Lord put you in it.
You pray that He get you out of it as soon
as possible.
You don't realize that He wants to talk to you and
wants you to learn something from the valley
experience.
What is the Lord teaching you?
Don't be too much in a hurry to get out of the
valley but use the time to reflect
and look within yourself.
In those valley experiences, it is sometimes very

difficult to pray, for you cannot focus, but if nothing else, seek Him and know that He loves you unconditionally, no matter what.

Know that you will get out of the valley, and when you do, it will be exhilarating to stand on the mountaintop and admire the view.

You'll come out of the valley experience more than a conqueror.

You'll feel refreshed and be a stronger person. So, thank the Lord for the valleys and look forward to the experience!

AND FINALLY, TO MY FELLOW TRAVELERS

It happens in the life of one who has faced abuse,
neglect, abandonment, and rejection;
A time comes when one must cross over to the
other side.
The "other side" represents a bright light—a ray
of hope—
From the restlessness, turmoil, confusion, anger,
and bitterness, to peace, tranquility,
and forgiveness.
It's time to pause and see that life cannot go on in
this way, for it is destructive to the self.
It's time to stop feeling sorry for oneself
and wallowing in self pity.
It's time to realize that the tears have been shed
and the well is dry.
A time comes for us to look beyond
and to see the reason for living.
It's time to stop focusing on self but rather on
what the experience has taught us.
It's time to see that life is passing by as we sit
there and keep asking questions like, "Why me?"
The bottom line is that it happened and that
cannot be erased.

Let's gain strength as we remember from Egypt
to the Promised Land went the children of Israel.
The Lord went with them as a pillar of cloud by
day and a pillar of fire by night.
His presence was always with them.
Even through this journey,
the Lord never forsook me.
It was hard to believe at times, and it was as
though I was in it alone.
I cried and cried, but now it is enough.
It's time for us to move on, because
He is always there.
He is our constant companion.
It took almost forty years for the children of Israel
to cross over; it has taken me twenty-two years—
No short cuts, but the long way.
One day I would think I had crossed over, but
then I realized that the process is a journey—
a long one.
Knowing who I am.
Knowing where I am going and knowing that
He has an awesome plan for my life.
Some days, I'm in the valleys, and on other days
on the highest mountain peaks.
Wondering if He is still there.
He whispers into my ear that He is with me as

He was with the children of Israel.
I question and seek answers,
which are not easily found.
But as I do so, I begin to get in touch with me—
who am I?
What am I to do while living on Earth?
I realize that I am not the only one who has been
in this predicament.
But many of us have been here, and we need to
touch one another—a word of encouragement,
a reason for living—because as iron sharpens
iron, we can sharpen one another.
We need to talk about our experiences
and move on.
I recognize that we serve a God
of second chances.
I realize that we are wonderfully
and fearfully made.
I know that we are a miracle,
and that He, the Almighty God, wants to use us.
But as crushed and broken vessels,
how can we hearken to His call?
He wants us to know that He loves us,
regardless, or in spite of, who we are or
what we have done.
With His unconditional love

He desires to see us go through.
But it takes a step on our part to run to the mercy
seat and find Him there with outstretched arms
to welcome us home and to pour His love on us.
He wants for us to come just as we are,
to tell Him what we are going through.
It takes a step of boldness and humility to
surrender all and to unburden the load.
It takes us to leave it at His feet, and in the
process get to know ourselves better.
And why we behave in certain ways or
speak certain things.
It takes honesty, some retrospection, and,
painful as it is, I rest assured that He is with us.
Things can only get better,
for one day we will cross the sea.
What seemed like a challenge once overcome will
be simple, because every step of the way
He is with us.
And when He is with us, nothing is impossible.
So, it is time to deal with reality, to acknowledge
that we have been hurt and that we are
still hurting.
That guilt, mistrust, anger, and bitterness,
we are prepared to deal with,
because we want to move forward.

We want to cross over but not on our own.
We tried on our own but have failed.
We grope for His hand,
holding it as a child holds the hand of her father.
First, we need to trust Him,
and that too is a challenge.
But it is a step at a time, small steps,
then as faith increases, they get bigger.
Then suddenly, at last we are crossing the sea.
And shouting victory,
for we are on the other side....

VII

As I write these concluding chapters, I want to share with you about the course that my life has taken, particularly after my season in Namibia. My story would not be complete if I did not discuss the other seasons in my life. My work-related successes and challenges as I took up a post as an international staff member; my relationships; the birthing of Daughters of Destiny groups and my climb up Mount Kilimanjaro have had a profound impact on the woman that I am. I was tested and tried in many situations and as I overcame, I was able to start shedding my fears and insecurities. It's almost as though, as the layers were being peeled off, I met what I did not know about myself - a strong woman, who I had grown to love. As we all know, painful and sad experiences are unavoidable but I had made the choice that they would not destroy me, but build me up so that I could climb to greater heights. There is always hope and out of something painful or sad, the Lord is more than able to turn it into something beautiful.

When I took my first international posting with the International Labour Organization (ILO) in Abidjan, there was no shadow of a doubt in many peoples' minds that that my Dad had tapped into his networks to help me. That was wrong information! My Dad was a man of principles and values. He never used his personal networks or connections to give any of his children breaks in life. My siblings and I are privileged to be where we are in our various stations in life because it has been through the sheer determination and belief in hard work that Dad instilled in us. He believed that you work hard to get to where you wanted to go and this is one of the lessons that I treasure. All of his accomplishments during his 75-year sojourn on this earth can be attributed to his hard work. I applied for my job on the internet and I was very pleasantly surprised to be short listed and interviewed for the post.

Taking up the posting in Abidjan was a wonderful opportunity for me to learn French. I had studied French in high school but regrettably, I hadn't taken my classes seriously so this was one of the major reasons that I had applied for the post as Decent Work Focal Point Officer in the Regional Office. At the time I did not know what it entailed, but with my work experience on HIV/AIDS, socio-economic and agriculture issues, Decent Work sounded like an interesting concept I was looking forward to learning more about.

I had been told a lot of positive things about Abidjan, that it was the most advanced city in West Africa and that the people were really welcoming. I was excited and had great expectations for my assignment. I landed in Abidjan and it was a totally new experience with the West African region. I was confronted by the hot and humid weather and being a girl from the Maluti Mountains in Lesotho, I did not know how to cope with the fact that I was sticky and wet most of the time. Air conditioning was a necessity but again it was artificial so I was always challenged to get the climate just right. I also soon figured that I needed to learn to negotiate when purchasing fruits and vegetables from the market stalls. In Maseru and Windhoek, we were spoiled and purchased literally everything from the supermarkets, so combining my poor negotiation skills and shaky French made shopping a chore. Getting around in taxis was not easy because it meant that I had to know some basic French words, so I often carried my dictionary and quickly learned to say 'droit' and 'gauche' which mean left and right respectively. The city was busy with people day and night, unlike Maseru and Windhoek, where after 18h00, the city becomes deathly quiet. People would move to the residential areas but in Abidjan, the residential homes and businesses seemed to be one and the same thing.

Adjusting to the job was also another maze and just trying to understand what I was supposed to do was overwhelming. I was often reminded of those puzzles in which you are supposed to find a path for the mouse to follow to get to the cheese. There are roadblocks at every turn but eventually, you find a way to lead the mouse to the cheese. This is what I went through and I would not be surprised to learn that many employees of the UN go through such experiences and can relate to mine. The UN organizations tend to be labyrinths. Well-coordinated and comprehensive induction programmes are really vital to assist prospective staff members to get on board, rather than for them to learn by trial and error. I had a job description which was generic but did not detail the specific tasks as the Decent Work Focal Point Officer.

The organization had come up with the concept of decent work which placed emphasis on the availability of employment in conditions of freedom, equity, security and human dignity. Seemingly my task was to understand its application from an African perspective. I sought guidance on what was expected from me but it was not forthcoming. It seemed that many of my colleagues were also grappling with understanding the concept, so it was difficult to give me guidance and they were caught up in their own jobs. In addition, being new to the ILO, with its tripartite structure and grasping concepts of social protection and labour standards, which were aspects of decent work was daunting. The only part that was a little clearer to me was the employment pillar but the rest was, as they say, all Greek to me. It took months of reading and working closely with colleagues to begin to understand the organization that I worked for and its mandate.

Settling in a new country and job exposed me to awkward issues related to relocation. When I was a child my family moved to Rome- where we lived for eight years- my Dad naturally dealt with all the details. But now on my own, I had to work out what it meant to be on mission status for three months and hardship allowances, so it was one question after another to those who had been working in the UN much longer than me. I understood that, while I was looking for a house, I was entitled to allowances that would cater for my staying in temporary furnished short-term accommodations and that a hardship allowance would be paid to compensate me for the difficult living conditions in the country where I was based. Looking for suitable accommodation, purchasing the basic essentials while waiting for my personal effects to arrive from South Africa were new issues to me. I waited for about four months before my furniture and other items arrived.

I was told that with the tense political situation in Abidjan at that time, it was not the same place that it used to be. I was made to understand that prior to the political upheavals it was the place to be. I could see the signs of a city that once was bustling with life. Even trying to find a place to meet other Christians and to plug in to be part of a church community was a challenge. After asking around, I eventually found a church, which I was told had many expatriates and that I would fit in. And since this was a very important aspect for me, I looked forward to being made welcome and to finding a home group, where a small number of us church members could gather during the week. However, when I got to the church, I was informed that many of the church members had been staff members from the African Development Bank, which had relocated to Tunisia. There was a small group of expatriates but I did not manage to make any connections. Needless to say, I continued to go to church and once the service was over, I would have to have a plan lined up, which mostly entailed spending much time on my own. Since this was something I had done when I was in Namibia and particularly, while I was writing the first edition of the book, 'Joy Comes in the Morning', it meant that I had come to love my own company, so I spent much time journaling, praying and reading. When I traveled out of Abidjan, I made sure that I stocked up on my reading materials. I was not motivated nor did I have the courage to look for places where foreigners hung out. I was still trying to figure out the West African scene. I did not regret my moving to Abidjan and accepted that it was bad timing, so I had to look for the positives. It was not easy but I knew that, like all things 'This season too would come to pass.'

Two months after my personal effects arrived in Abidjan, we were evacuated to Addis Ababa. I just locked up the apartment and left with two suitcases and that was it. Whether I would ever return to Abidjan was neither here or there. What would be the fate of my personal effects was a mystery. Luckily, I had not put too much value on my material possessions, except there were certain items that had sentimental attachments. This included my framed pictures and paintings from the different countries

I had lived in and traveled to; my books; my photo albums with memories from my college years, trips that I had taken with my family and with friends; and gifts that had been given to me. This included Mongo, my stuffed big white rabbit with large floppy ears, which my brother gave me when he first visited me in college in 1986. Mongo had been everywhere I had been. The loss of these items would be sad because they were irreplaceable

Although the trip to Addis was smooth and uneventful, it was not one of those trips that I was thrilled about because it was not by choice that we had to be in Addis. Six months prior to this trip, I had participated in a meeting in Addis, so I knew what to expect in terms of the office and where we would be located. What concerned me was that I did not know about the hotel and the day-to-day living in Addis. It was like no other African city that I had ever visited. It was a city of contrasts with poverty and wealth existing side by side and a people I could not clearly figure out. In a number of instances, I felt an element of racism targeted towards other Africans and being looked down upon. When I was at a restaurant with my Caucasian friends, the Ethiopian waiters or waitresses would focus their attention on my friends and I would almost be an afterthought. Whether this was because they thought they were superior to me or they were inferior, I could not tell you. One thing that I admired about Ethiopians is that they are proud of their heritage and cling to their traditions and culture. Addis is one of those cities that you have to discover for yourself and one needs to form one's own impressions.

A friend of mine who lived in Addis said that you either hate or love Addis. For me, it was not an either or situation because there were aspects of living in Addis that I appreciated and others that I disliked.

When we arrived at the hotel, my initial impression was 'Oops, this place is not going to be my temporary home'. One could see that in the past it had been a classy hotel but it now needed some major renovation and I would not be in Addis long enough to see it happening. My impressions and views were shared by my colleagues, and so we all started looking for other options. I knew that I had to be comfortable and it did not matter how much it would cost me. The Hilton was strategically placed, within walking distance to the office and Meskel Square and Ghion Hotel, which has wonderful gardens in which to spend a Sunday afternoon; also, there was a supermarket at the hotel; a heated swimming pool, a gym and a number of restaurants. I opted to stay in a studio at the Hilton hotel for six months and it was a good place to be.

At work, I continued to seek guidance on my expected role and contribution to the office. Since this guidance was not in the offing, difficult as it was for me, I had to come to terms with the reality and understanding that the management had bigger decisions to address in an unanticipated situation. They had to look for solutions for staff members, in terms of safety and where the Regional Office would be relocated, the cost implications and so on. It meant that issues had to be dealt with one step at a time.

I was told that I needed to come up with my own understanding and interpretation of my position and to develop a work plan. Now you talk about taking a novice and throwing them in the deep end of the pool and tell them to swim was exactly how I felt. I recalled another time, when I landed in Windhoek and started working for the Namibian Economic Policy and Research Unit (NEPRU), where my job description was very clear and this had helped to quickly understand my role in the broader vision of the institution.

After fumbling here and there and entertaining pity parties about the work environment that I loathed because I was unclear about my role and my added value, I opened the door to low self-esteem and low self-worth. These were not doors that I wanted to open because they took me back to believing that I was a failure, emotions that I struggled so much with after I was sexually abused. I had to constantly speak and remind myself of the milestones that I had achieved from the time that I had decided to deal with abuse to the point where I had reached.

I did not understand what the Lord was up to and why after such a short stay in Abidjan, I was evacuated to Addis Ababa. Why had things happened this way? I found no answers to my questions. As I mulled over my situation, I was reminded of a day when three pastors, who were the President and Vice-Presidents of Haggai Institute Namibia had called me to their office to appreciate my contribution as a Board member and to bid me farewell with a prayer. Immediately after the prayer, one of the pastors told me that he had received a prophetic word from the Lord that there was going to be great chaos in my life. He said that the only way that I would overcome was to rely and lean on the Lord.

The Abidjan and Addis scenarios were clearly evidence of chaos to me and indeed, I had to spend time praying and asking God to direct my footsteps and to give me grace for each day. I would be lying if I said that on some days, I wasn't so discouraged and disillusioned that I had to pray against such emotions because they were not going to help, given the situation at hand. I even thought that I could avoid going through whatever I was meant to go through and started to explore ways of leaving the job. I wanted out and if there was a short-cut to something, which I thought was better, I'd have fled. Fortunately that was not God's plan for me and so, despite sending out several applications for various posts in diverse organizations, I did not get any responses. As time went, I chastised myself that I needed to smell the coffee beans. I had not completed my probationary period, so who on earth would offer me a position at this point? And also what would a prospective employer think of me? Deep inside, I knew that even though I did not want to entertain the thought, God was perfecting me. I would call home and share my situation with Mom and Dad, hoping that they would sympathize with me but instead they would encourage me to persevere and to just keep the faith because God knew why He had placed me in the organization.

Running helped to keep me in good spirits. I would run along the streets of Addis but once the dreaded rainy season kicked in, I had to go to the gym, which is not my favorite. I loved running outside because I could forget about my troubles and appreciate and admire the sights, the sounds and the smells around me. I would see the boy leading a herd of goats along the main street to the market; the beggar rousing from sleep on the side of the road; the sun rising on a crisp morning; the clouds building up and ready to burst before I got home; other runners and walkers; and cars driven by men, who slowed down just a little bit to get a good look at the face, which came with the shapely body.

Studying was one of my pastimes, so a year before I left Namibia, I enrolled in an Honors Degree in Psychology with the University of South Africa (UNISA). Since I was not a Psychology major, I had to do third year courses, which I completed in Namibia. By the time, I got to Abidjan I was ready to begin the Honors programme, which took two years to complete. Why had I opted to pursue Psychology? I wanted to understand why people do what they do and this could have been linked to the fact that while I was going through my journey of healing from sexual abuse, I needed to understand why I did what I did. The psychology course was fascinating and I really enjoyed it. I could relate with some of the content since I had unknowingly applied psychology principles to help myself. I was glad that I was on the right track and attributed this to the wisdom that the Lord imparted to me. I also felt that this course would come handy in the workplace and when I mentored young women. I felt that I was building for the future and doing the course was a good distraction. When I wanted to get into pity party mode, I would search for reading materials, read them and do my assignments.

I chose my friends selectively because I wanted to be around people who were positive and would add value to my life and to whose I could also make a contribution. I shied away from groups where we would complain and moan about our circumstances and talk about other people. When I associated with such company, I would not be in high spirits and that was when I would be prone to negative thoughts and attitudes. I am not a great TV fan, I would rather read a good book or be writing assignments or updating my journal. So, even when I was in Addis, I maintained this philosophy. Some of the best assignments for my Psychology course were submitted while I was in Addis. One lesson I learned was when life gives me blows, which will happen, it's so critical for me to direct my energy and time to goals that are worth pursuing and not on those that leave me worse off.

With all that was happening in my life, I felt the need to find a church family and after asking around at work, colleagues told me about the International Pentecostal Church (IPC). One Sunday, I attended their service and immediately I was well received by the pastor, his family and church members. That church became my spiritual home and I became active in various activities, which allowed me to make new friends. I enjoyed being a part of the church. The joy that I had lost by not belonging to a church family in Abidjan and during the move from Abidjan to Addis was soon restored.

Being the friendly person that I am, I soon forged a couple of good relationships with Ethiopian colleagues in the office, who inducted me into the world of appreciating Ethiopian cuisine. Over lunches, we would go and eat 'injera' (a yeast-risen flatbread, traditionally made out of teff flour with a unique, slightly spongy texture and sour taste) and we would have good laughs about what was happening in the office. I felt that that I was part of a network of pleasant and like-minded colleagues and this was positive.

I also made a decision to change my attitude to one of being grateful for my blessings rather than dwelling on what I did not have. I had to be thankful that I had a job in which I had an opportunity to carve out what I wanted to do, I was safe and had somewhere comfortable to sleep every night, and I had good colleagues. I had to remind myself that in all that I was going through, God had a purpose and God had not made a mistake by taking me to Addis. So, when those pity parties would come, I would read and reflect on the poem that I wrote about pity parties. I decided to be pro-active and to see what I could do in the workplace. I learned about colleagues' various areas of specialization and when I finally identified a gap, I proceeded to define a niche for myself because no one was going to do it for me. I learned that at the end of the day, I am responsible for my life and I play a role in shaping it. Even though I was depending on management to guide me, when that did not happen, I had a choice to sit back and cry about it or to do something about it. I opted for the latter, even though it took some time to get to that point. One thing, I learned from my experience was that I would do as much as possible to assist newcomers into the ILO. If I ever found myself in a supervisory or management role, I would sit with a staff member and chart out the tasks and what is expected from them. On a regular basis, we would discuss how the staff member is executing their tasks. There is no need for anyone to be stumbling to find their place when there are people, like myself, who would have gone through experiences that could benefit others. Instead of being caught up in our own roles, it's a good thing to share and guide others, especially those who are newcomers in the UN system.

My time in Addis came to an end after six months and I then headed to Geneva, still as the Decent Work Focal Point Officer working in the Regional Office for Africa. I would be working out of Geneva until a new country location was identified. Still not quite clear on what lay ahead, I certainly knew that I still had to go and find my place and purpose, more so in Geneva. I knew that it would still take extra doses of believing in me, which was a test of endurance and required willpower, elements that I would tap on later to help me through my climb to Uhuru Peak on Mt. Kilmanjaro.

The fourteen months that I lived in Geneva were an eye-opener. It was an experience to be in a city, where almost everything worked like a clock, the buses came on time, the shops would open and close exactly on time, people rarely smiled and everyone minded their own business. This was a contrast to the smiling faces that I had gotten accustomed to in Africa. My hypothesis is that the sun has a lot to do with our smiling faces in Africa. When the sun shines, everyday, how can you not be smiling and laughing all the time? Also we are more relaxed and laid back when it comes to keeping time. One of the challenges of living in Geneva was when winter came, it would be dark for a number of days and I would really miss seeing the sun.

I lived in a hotel and then in serviced apartments for five months, since it was close to impossible to find accommodation in Geneva. I got to see a lot of the city as I trudged up and down to view apartments. I would indicate interest and then to be told days later that the apartment was no longer vacant. Just when I was ready to give up, I found a furnished, pleasant one bedroom apartment that was located within walking distance to Cornavin (the train station) and affordable by Geneva standards. After my Abidjan and Addis experience, and now that I knew that I would be in Geneva for fourteen months meant that I could settle down, in terms of creating a home. Even though I still had many unanswered questions, I was now more focused on what I needed to do in terms of my job; my prayers also changed from those where I was seeking answers to those where I expressed my thanks to the Lord

The work situation changed for the positive in Geneva since this time, I knew that I had to carve out what I had to do. I was still the Decent Work Focal Point Officer and so I made contact with other colleagues working in the relevant Unit and got insights on how they were approaching the issue of Decent Work from the global perspective. I looked at the concept from Africa's perspective and started extrapolating elements that would feed into the work of my colleagues in the Regional Programming Unit. They appreciated the inputs and it added value to our work. As I drew from my research and analytical skills, colleagues in the Unit at Headquarters would request for my inputs and finally, I thought "Yes, girl way to go..." At the same time, I decided to be a sponge and absorb what was cast my way. I did not shy away from any opportunity to do a work-related task that was unfamiliar because I figured that was the fastest way to learn. A work-related mission to Bangkok exposed me to how the Decent Work Agenda was being applied in Asia. Interacting and engaging and sharing lessons with colleagues gave me new ideas of the possibilities that lay with the Decent Work concept.

While I was gaining a better understanding on the Decent Work concept, youth employment was emerging as an issue of great concern in Africa. I was fortunate to be in Geneva at the time of the International Labour Conference that is held in June and had youth employment as one of its thematic discussions. I was asked to coordinate and compile stories and good practices from the various country offices in Africa. I also sat in a number of meetings that were preparing for the conference. This exposed me to the topic and I got to know who worked on what, when it came to youth employment issues. This network would prove to be helpful when I eventually moved back to Addis. During the conference, I attended different sessions and acquired greater understanding of youth employment and how regions other than Africa were addressing it. I was thrilled when it was proposed that I shift roles to be the regional coordinator on youth employment. I like structure and tend to work better when I am clear on boundaries and this was a very specific assignment. Even though I had to articulate my tasks, it was simple for me since such a regional post existed in Asia and I could borrow elements from it.

When I was in Geneva, even though it was a brief stay I was also afforded the opportunity to appreciate how the ILO worked. I was able to understand the bigger picture of the organization: how the country offices fit into the Regional Office and how that relates to the Office in Geneva was helpful knowledge in terms of also placing my own contribution. By sitting in the Governing Body meetings, which are held twice a year, I was able to witness first-hand the format that discussions take between the ILO and the workers, employers and Ministries of Labour. Unlike other UN agencies, where their counterpart is only one Government Ministry, ILO is accountable to the three groups mentioned above.

I had no dull moments in Geneva and so there was little time to dwell on what I did not have. I did not have to look for distractions because in a city such as Geneva, where there are people from all corners of the world working in several UN agencies, embassies and multinational companies, there is much to do. The city is teeming with plenty of shops, which would be luring to me to spend my money, but thank God that I am not an avid shopper. I am also not one to window shop since I quickly get bored, so I tend to go shopping only when I need to buy something. I had activities, twice a month with the Daughters of Destiny (which I will tell more about in the last chapter), and I participated in meetings of the Toastmasters Club (it promotes communication and leadership skills) and I was exploring a number of friendships. As I made new friends, I also kept the old friends. Since Geneva was an exciting destination, a very good friend of mine from Lesotho came over to visit me. The spring and summer months were my favorite because I could spend more time outdoors. I thoroughly enjoyed my morning runs in the park, taking in the beauty of the blooming flowers or admiring Lake Geneva. It was during those moments when I was admiring nature that I felt so privileged to be alive.

The successful completion of my Honors degree in Psychology called for much focus, which I was able to muster. It was another accomplishment to have another degree up my sleeve. I decided not to proceed to doing a Masters degree because I needed a break from meeting deadlines and working on assignments. I felt that I had better enjoy Geneva since one day- and it would be soon- I would have to leave to go to another country.

In the meantime, a decision had been taken by the ILO that the Regional Office would be located in Addis Ababa. By January

2006, all Regional Office staff members would move to Addis and that included me. This time, I was more positive about going back to Addis, I knew what to expect and in terms of my assignment, it was clear what I was going to do. Since I was going to be there longer than fourteen months, I could look for a house and not have to live in a hotel. Also, I looked forward to seeing my personal effects for the first time after Abidjan. I never had the chance to return to Abidjan so I had to ask a colleague to help me to pack up everything, which she faithfully did. My personal effects remained in storage in France for almost a year and then when I was relocated to Addis this time, they were shipped there.

Returning to a place where I had been before made a great difference. I also met up with a Mosotho friend, whom I had met when I had first started working at the Ministry of Agriculture in Lesotho. We had struck a friendship that endured the distances and it was a pleasant surprise to learn that she had moved to work in the Lesotho Embassy. When I contacted her, she asked me to stay with her and kindly hosted me until I found my own place. Staying with her was great and if anything, it also strengthened the bond between us. I returned to the church where I had been going to previously and most of the folk were delighted to have me once again in their midst. It was like going back home to family and taking off from where I had left. I soon found a pleasant house with a small, well-manicured garden and had to wait about a month before my personal effects arrived. It did not take me too long to settle and to be surrounded by familiar things.

I inherited a gardener cum guard, who barely spoke any English, but he was a good man and very protective of me. When I would go running or walk to the nearby shops, he would be anxiously waiting for me. I also had a very pleasant, reliable and dependable helper who would do a good job to keep my house spic and span. It was good to be surrounded by caring people and this contributed to my smoothly settling in Addis after my circuitous route from Windhoek to Abidjan to Addis to Geneva.

I thoroughly enjoyed my assignment as the Youth Employment Specialist. After coming up with specific tasks that I shared with my supervisor, I came up with a work plan. Several African countries sought assistance with their youth employment initiatives so that entailed me traveling extensively. I learned that there were several initiatives to address youth employment but they were not well documented and so the initiatives tended to remain small and isolated. Different country experiences could be shared, and one way I brought about that connection was by initiating a quarterly newsletter. I also collaborated with other Specialists working on issues, such as the Microfinance and Gender, as a way to address youth employment in an integrated manner. I don't think that it was by coincidence that I was drawn to youth employment but working with and on issues for young people is my passion. Each day, I would wake up with enthusiasm and ideas filled my mind on what I could do.

When you have a job that you are passionate about, success is inevitable. You can only excel when you do what you love.

Even my confidence level soared as I became an expert and was sought out for my knowledge and advice. My rather shaky first years in the organization seemed like they had taken place many eons ago and I could see that I had to go through that season in order to arrive at the place where I now was. Most infants crawl before they can start walking and it is at certain stages when this happens. Imagine what might have happened if I had not gone through this experience? The Lord is in the business of building character and once I had gone through the experience, I was not the same person. It's so critical to persevere to the end of a task. Sometimes the end seems so far away, and so it seemed for Uhuru Peak, when I climbed Mount Kilimanjaro. At one point I was ready to give up, but I was so close and it was not the time to give up. So, I persevered and I thank God that I did. The same applies if I had been persistent in my efforts to leave the ILO; I would never have had the privilege of working with youth issues. I am also thankful for those who entrusted me with this very important portfolio.

One of the highlights of my stay in Addis was that my hard work was recognized and I received a promotion. The promotion did not come as a surprise; I was expecting it, in the sense that I had worked so hard and my supervisor and other colleagues regularly valued my contributions. I was delighted to have received it. A friend of mine purchased me a bouquet of assorted roses to say 'Well done!' My parents were very happy for me and Dad expected nothing less from his daughter and was very proud.

Even if I had wanted to celebrate the attainment of my promotion, I could not since I received the good news a day before my departure to climb Mount Kilimanjaro. My mind had switched off from work issues and I was now filled with thoughts of 'How is it going to be and will I get to the top?' The promotion was timely and there would be great reason to celebrate, especially if I managed to summit, to reach Uhuru Peak. It never crossed my mind that Tanzania would be my next duty station. God works in mysterious ways and His ways are surely not our ways...

Upon my return from climbing Mount Kili, (more about that it in a later chapter), a competition for job vacancies was launched. Two Deputy Director positions, one in Dar es Salaam and the other in Pretoria were advertised. I was not planning to apply for any of the positions since I was enjoying working on youth employment issues- I felt that there was still so much for me to contribute to the field. Several colleagues at different times approached me, saying that I should apply for one of the positions since a management position in a country office would expose me to another perspective on the workings of the organization. I told them that the youth employment portfolio was still of great interest but they reasoned that even in the Deputy Director position, I could still work in that area. After toying with the idea, and not quite sure if I was making the right decision and taking the right step, I went ahead and applied for both jobs. I figured that the only way that I would find out if I liked a management position was to go ahead and if I was successful, to try it.

In addition, I would get to see how the ILO worked at the country level versus at regional level, which had been my experience since joining the organization.

I was more attracted to working in Tanzania, given that I had never worked in any of the other three countries, Kenya, Uganda and Somalia which the office covered. I was also interested in working in a country where the UN was piloting on how it could contribute to national development goals as one UN and not as different UN agencies. So, instead of having several different programmes for the many UN agencies, there would be One UN programme. One of the main objectives was to introduce, to the extent possible, an efficient and effective mechanism whereby national counterparts would deal with one UN and not several different organizations. In addition, a number of personal reasons drew me to Tanzania, Dad had worked in Tanganyika in 1956; then when he worked for FAO, he was responsible for the Tanzania programme and I had read about the 'Ujamaa villages' so I was interested to learn more about the people and the country. Some of our best friends when we lived in Rome were from Tanzania, so this would be a good opportunity to look for them and see what had become of them. Working in Pretoria sounded good but since I had worked in Southern Africa before, it did not grab my hopes quite as much.

When I was informed that I was the successful candidate for the post of Deputy Director in Dar es Salaam I had mixed feelings. I was happy that the Office had confidence in me and excited to be going to a new office and city but I also had some anxiety.

It did not feel like when I left Lesotho to go and work in Namibia, where I knew that the job had been tailor made for me. In this instance, there was some uncertainty, maybe because I was going to give up some of the control and autonomy that I had while I was coordinating and managing the youth employment portfolio. Also, I had fears about once again being in a situation where my roles would not be clear, given that the Deputy Director position included diverse aspects such as programme coordination; financial management; human resources management; engagement with other UN agencies and other related functions. I had no doubt that I would do a good job because I knew my capabilities, and once I set myself to a task I try as much as possible to do it well. However, what I was not sure about was whether the fit was right and if I would enjoy the diverse aspects of the job. I was not worried about the office that I was going to work in because during my previous missions, I had sensed that it was a positive environment. I set aside my fears and decided that I would see once I got to Dar.

Eventually, the time came for me to leave Addis and it was hectic. Deciding on what to take and what to leave behind, both in my house and at the office; when the packers should come; selling my car; spending time with the Daughters and trying to fit in dinners with friends was exhausting. I didn't realize until I was leaving that I had forged so many friendships and Daughter relationships. And as some of you know, saying 'goodbye' is not easy but since I had said them many times, I lived in the hope that our paths would cross again and since we were living in a world of technology, we should be able communicate relatively easily. Since I have lived in so many different places, I do work on keeping in touch with people through emails, text messages and telephone. My feeling is that if I want to maintain relationships, they need to be nurtured but it takes two people to do so and I often have to remind my friends. But when being busy creeps in, as it did with me, keeping in touch becomes a challenge and friendships are compromised. It's so easy to drift apart and that's a sad phenomena. When once you had so much to talk about, before you know it, little is said. As people change and go through different life experiences, the sharing becomes less and soon the emails begin to trickle and then sadly, the friendship dies a natural death.

My settling into Dar es Salaam was much easier than in the other countries, and maybe this was attributed to the fact that once you have done this moving around the world business a number of times you learn the tricks of the game. After about six weeks, I identified a place that I liked the minute I saw it. Luckily, the apartment was partially furnished, so I was comfortable at the outset and from almost all the rooms, I had a view of the ocean, which was exactly what I wanted. My personal effects came after four months, and then I truly settled in with my familiar things around me. At night I sleep to the sound of the waves crashing on the shore. Most of the time, I have a lovely sea breeze. And over the weekends, when I am at home, I stand on the balcony and my gaze stretches for miles over the ocean. From time to time I see the ships, slowly moving to the harbour and I ask myself where they came from and what they brought. In the mornings, I wake up early to run and most of the time I run on the main road but I take in the smells, sounds and sights of the ocean. I say a prayer of thanks to the Lord for affording me this opportunity, which might be the last one to live in a country where I have such proximity to the ocean.

Dar is an easy city to settle in and it was like coming to familiar ground, in that I could relate better to Tanzanians, in terms of culture and language since Kiswahili is a Bantu language and there are a few words that are similar to Sesotho. I was surprised at how few people speak English and that posed a problem for me. Learning and speaking languages is not one of my strengths. I accept that we have all been given certain gifts but maybe, I just do not have the interest and do not make the time to learn a language. In the countries that I have lived, I have managed to get by with a few basic words. The only language which I have invested my efforts and time has been French and I am still determined to learn it.

The cuisine is most palatable and I am enthralled by the variety of fruits and vegetables that Tanzania has to offer – the sweet, luscious mangoes, the sweet papaya and bananas, and the fleshy avocados, to name a few, are just so divine. Since I am a vegetarian and eat only seafood, Dar is the right place for me with tasty, fleshy and fresh fish at my disposable all the time.

The city is one of contrasts, like most African cities where you find on the one hand artificial neighborhoods where the expatriate community lives and then on the other hand, neighborhoods where the locals live. The two worlds do not always mix and the tendency is to have the divisions of 'them' and 'us.' When you mention where you live, it's almost as though a barrier goes up and people have already preconceived notions, which you are either forced to dispel or just accept that people are entitled to their own views. I have gotten used to people having preconceived notions about me and realize that it is one of those things that I must live with. Growing up in Lesotho with a Dad that was in public office, for most of his life meant that once you introduced yourself to people, they would always say 'Ah, the daughter of Dr. Phororo...' and now, that I am an international staff member, its 'Oh, you are ...' This makes it difficult for spontaneous relationships to evolve because I have first to deal with letting people see beyond my position and status and to see the true Hops.

Two main shocks that I had when I arrived in Dar were the traffic jams and the amount of time that I would spend in the car, stuck in traffic. In Addis, there had been lots of traffic but it moved and the jams were not on a daily basis. I also could not get over the power outages that were the order of the day. However, I learned to live with the traffic jams and just made sure that I have good gospel music playing in the car and those are times when I reflect on issues. Thank God for generators, when the power goes off but of course, it does not come free, so that is an additional diesel cost.

From the minute that I landed in the office, it was one thing after another. I had never been so busy in my life. I work long hours and some days are particularly challenging, as I am in several meetings and then there are the payment requests to be signed, payments to be authorized and released, performance appraisals to provide inputs and the hundreds of emails that have to be read. I was so overwhelmed at the beginning and for several months I was at a loss as I searched for ways to cope. Since the Office covered three other countries, I had to take extensive two to three day missions which were tiring and yet they afforded a good opportunity to touch base with colleagues and our partners. Then, there were the other tasks that I had to do as Officer in Charge and this included representing the office at functions. I would get tongue-tied and not know what on earth to say to the Minister or to the President.

I have now consoled myself that the issues that I grapple with as a Deputy Director are endemic to others who are also Deputy Directors. I have learned that being a Deputy Director requires humility, good communication and persuasion skills to get people to do what you want, and that it's important to listen and find out what is going around you. Finding a balance to be able to cover the several areas of my responsibilities and focus on what I do well is also necessary. Figuring what to do and how to do it comes with the job and is something you have to learn on the job. Little by little and with each passing day, I learned how and what I need to do for my job to be less stressful.

Eight months after I arrived in Dar and six weeks after we had laid my Dad to rest, I was involved in a head-on collision that wrecked my car beyond repair. One bright Wednesday morning, I had just run, and I was on that post-exercise euphoric high and just praising the Lord for being alive. That morning, I had reflected on the events of the past few months and when I imagined how Dad would have loved to run in Dar. He and Mom had plans to visit me but for him, it was not meant to be. I got into my car, locked the door, fastened my seat belt and headed off to work. As I was driving, I noticed a pick-up tailing me and the driver was determined to overtake me. Finally, he managed to pass me but only to crash into my car, minutes later, at a four way intersection where I had the right of way. When we got to the four way intersection, like any well trained driver, I expected him to stop so I continued driving, but at the high speed at which he was driving, he did not stop. I said to myself, "He's going to hit me." I was so helpless at that moment and I just surrendered all to the Lord. There was no way that I could avoid him and before I knew it he had driven into me with a bang, hitting the left passenger side. Given the impact of the collision, my airbags inflated, the car was buffeted to the right and then came swinging to the left and flipped over to rest on the passenger's side. As all this was happening, I realized that I was saying "Jesus, Jesus, Jesus!" I know that Jesus came to my rescue. People ran to my car, they tried to open the door to get me out and I calmly remembered that I had locked the door. I unlocked it, and they tried to pull me out but they were hurting me. Then I reminded them that I still had my seat belt on. I undid the seat belt and they pulled me out. Thank God that I had fastened my seatbelt or I could have been thrown out of the windshield and I didn't want to imagine what could have happened then. At this point a crowd had gathered and I was told later that those who witnessed the accident feared that I had not survived because of the force of the impact.

They laid me on the side of the road and I tried to locate any pain in my body by stretching but I couldn't sense any pain, although I felt shaken up. Minutes later my colleagues, who were luckily running late to the office spotted my car and came to assist. With a calmness that I can only say came from the Lord, I requested that they get my handbag since I had heard horror stories that when accidents happen, people rush to the scene, not necessarily to assist but to see what they can loot. That said, my bag, which was my concern was salvaged. A doctor passing on her way to work stopped to see if she could assist and advised that I should not be moved since internal injuries could have taken place and it was better that I be moved by the paramedics. A policeman came to the scene, and he took a statement and then my car was towed away. As I was driven to the hospital in the ambulance, tears trickled down my face as I thought of what could have been and I knew that it was not yet my time to go and join my beloved Pops.

I thanked the Lord for His protection and presence in my life and I knew that He worked it all out for me such that He would send my colleagues at exactly that time. It was not by coincidence but it was the way the Lord planned it. I prayed that even though the enemy meant the accident for evil, it would be to the glory of the Lord's Name. The doctor insisted on taking extensive x-rays to ensure that I had no internal injuries but by this time, I had let go and trusted the Lord that I was fine. I was sent home with pain killers since I sustained only bruises. What a miracle...

When my car was towed to the office, colleagues could not believe that I got away with just bruises and they said that for sure, God was with me. The car was written off. I claimed the insurance and subsequently purchased another car. I purchased the new car online from Japan. I was eager to have it come soon since I had to rely on taxis to get around, which was inconvenient. When the company had shipped the car and it was still making its trip to Dar, they sent me the shipping documents and I later found out that they had shipped out the wrong car. It was exactly the same colour, was manufactured in the same year, had less mileage and was more expensive due to options- such as a sunroof and indicators on the side lights- than the car that I had ordered. It was so good to get an email from my sales representative telling me that management had taken the decision that I would get the car at the same price. I was in awe of God and how He worked.

After the accident occurred, I reflected on why it happened so soon after Pops passed on. A friend said that when misfortune strikes, it strikes hard as the course of events had demonstrated. I preferred to believe that what I had experienced was what life is all about. Living life has its highs and lows and the Lord has fashioned us so that we can go through them. He builds character so that we can be what He wants us to be. I believe that after having been through sexual abuse, I can go through anything. And God allows certain things to come our way because He knows how much each one of us can handle. He knows what we need to go through before He promotes us to a higher level. I have no regrets about what has happened in my life because if I had not gone through the trials, I would not be the woman that I am today. When people look at me, they see a strong woman, but they just don't know what I have been through. One of my Daughters often says that she wants to be like me because I am such a strong woman. The question is, would she want to go through the experiences that I have been through to be the woman I am? Maybe she would not. Rarely do we think that people are who they are because of what life has cast their way.

I also have learned that as one progresses up the career ladder, it can be one heck of a lonely journey. People don't really know how to treat you and they expect you to behave in a certain way and have reached so many conclusions about you. In order to make people comfortable, it means that you have to go the extra mile to prove to people that you are not who they might think that you are. I am just Hops, a normal human being, who just happens to be occupying the position of Deputy Director. Whenever I go home for holidays, I am always amused when people remark that I have not changed. Why on earth would being a Deputy Director change me? I guess they expected me to no longer go and look them up when I was home, or that I'd have no time to listen to what is happening in their lives. Maybe, they expected me to dress and walk in a certain manner, I don't know. I'd remind them that it's only a position, which can change overnight. We have heard stories of those who rose to great heights and walked over everyone and then overnight their situations changed. With a crash, like Humpty Dumpty they fell down. Needless to say, I do sometimes get tired of having to prove that I am just Hops and so, now I figure out that people who want to know me will find out if they really want to.

Another workplace issue that I have had to confront is related to the fact that I am a petite woman. I have always been very comfortable with my size and I have never thought about it as being an issue. In the ILO, notably men have remarked that I need to get 'fuller' or I need 'more meat' because that is how African men like their women. I wonder how African men liking their women has anything to do with the workplace, unless of course, it means that they will have little respect and are unlikely to listen to the views of a petite woman. Girlfriends have also advised me to put on some weight if I want to be taken seriously. So, imagine this scenario? I gain weight to be taken seriously! There is something fundamentally wrong with that kind of thinking. Being big has nothing to do with being taken seriously. Forget that. I will not go against my principles just to be accepted. It's how the woman carries out her duties, how she communicates and her deportment that are most important. What matters is that I am comfortable and accept myself just as I am. If men or women have problems with my being petite, that is not my problem.

It's so entertaining and I enjoy observing the dynamics of how people behave and treat me when they don't know me. I recall one incident where I was being introduced as the Deputy Director for the first time. This incident links a little bit to my previous point. I was escorted by another colleague, who was bigger in size. As we waited for the lady whom we had gone to pay a courtesy call, she finally came and she did not know who the Deputy was. She gave me one glance and automatically deduced that the Deputy had to be my colleague and maybe, thought that I was probably an assistant who was going to capture the notes from the meeting. Just as she was getting ready to do the welcome and formalities, which were addressed to my colleague, the latter gave her the eye and told her that I was the Deputy. You should have seen her face, it was shock, then embarrassment and then she welcomed me to the office. She even mentioned that it was so encouraging for ILO to appoint young women in senior management positions. Deep in my heart, I had to stifle a giggle because I had taken her by surprise.

From men, I get some snide remarks and looks and sometimes, they even try to undermine me. There are some instances when I let things go for there are some battles that are not worth fighting at all. But there are other times when it's important for me to get my point across, so that I am taken seriously. However, I'd rather not go that way, which thankfully is not very often. But sometimes, for the record, I need to put things straight in no uncertain terms that I am an intelligent and capable woman and that I have earned my position and no-one has handed it over to me.

I have also learned that being nice does not always pay off, especially when you are dealing with bad attitude. Not that one wants to be confrontational but sometimes it is inevitable. However, it's very important to be assertive and to know thyself. If not, you will be pulled by the nose and do things that do not give you any peace. Sometimes, I get the impression that people are uncomfortable with women who seem to know what they want and do not conform. It seems that it is easier to be accepted when you do what others are doing but the minute you don't do what others are doing, your popularity dwindles. E.E. Cummings could not have put it any better, "To be nobody but yourself – in a world which is doing its best, night and day, to make you everybody else – it means to fight the hardest battle which any human being can fight and never stop fighting". Suddenly, no-one understands you and the majority will try to sway you so that you come to your senses and do what everyone else is doing. "What's wrong with her anyway?" they begin to ask and truth be told, "There's absolutely nothing wrong with her, she's just being herself." And for anyone to be themselves means to be unique. We are all created as unique beings with our various talents, personalities and gifts and that is why no person's experience can ever be the same as that of another. So, rather than stifle uniqueness, it is my hope that we encourage people that we know to be who they are meant to be.

One of the things that I have observed is that sadly, it's a man's world out there and men have established many networks that are critical for their upward mobility. The figures show that even though women are increasingly occupying more senior level positions, men are still leading. I believe that women need to do more on coming together to support each other rather than as we sometimes do, not doing things in our best interests and not wishing each other well. Women mentoring each other in work places is not a common scenario and its such a shame because those who have climbed the ladder have so much to teach others, who follow in their footsteps. Mentoring is a time consuming activity but in the absence of the networks that men are so good at carving out for themselves, what are our possibilities? I guess one of the reasons that it's inevitable is that many times, women in the positions that they hold are trying so hard to fight against the socio-cultural forces of being a woman, so just making the time and space to start mentoring others is a challenge. That said, I really do believe that there must be a way to get around it, such that when our own daughters get to the positions that we now occupy and higher ones, they will not have to be fighting the same battles that we are currently fighting. I do believe that one day we will get it right and be able to support each other as we progress upwards in our careers.

VIII

In a previous chapter, I recounted my struggle to grapple with love but at this stage in my life I have come to understand better what love is and allow myself to love and be loved. Love is one of the greatest experiences. It's a shame that it has been so cheapened in the world we live in. Notice the way people fall in and out of love, and the way they use the term so loosely. Imagine if the Lord also used it the way that we use it: where would we be? He loves us unconditionally and I believe that we, too, can choose to love unconditionally.

When I had just arrived in Abidjan to assume my first job with the Regional Office for Africa in the International Labour Organization (ILO), I was introduced to a man by a colleague. I was instantly attracted to him- not physically- but there was something about him that I liked yet could not pin down. I didn't do much to follow up on this attraction because I didn't have that kind of courage. However, since we both worked in international organizations that dealt with developmental issues, our paths crossed from time to time. And even then, our discussions would be limited to work-related topics. For the five months that I was in Abidjan, the political situation progressively worsened and soon I, with other ILO colleagues, was evacuated to Addis Ababa. I was in Addis for six months, and thereafter I was transferred to Geneva where I again met the man and worked closely with him. I did not entertain the thought of getting to know him better since one of the things that I had learned as a result of being abused was not to have any expectations about a man liking me. I never thought that I was good enough or attractive enough to be noticed by any man, even if there was a seed of attraction in me. I had learned to suppress those feelings. With time, I discovered that I could talk about diverse topics related to the development of the African continent with this man - not that we agreed on everything, but we could at least engage in lengthy and stimulating debates. We never ran out of topics to talk about and there were no dull moments, and this formed a strong basis for a great friendship. Also, I figured this was one of the things that attracted me to him. I have always found men with sharp and witty minds very appealing, maybe because it was one of the traits that I admired about my late Dad.

For me, just the experience of building a relationship with a man was a great achievement. With my previous relationships I had not made it this far, so I was quite proud of myself. In addition, a close girlfriend (who I had last seen almost thirty years before) confirmed to me that he was a good man and eliminated any shadow of doubt that I had. My friend and I attended the same secondary school in Maseru and we had been good friends until my family left to go to Rome. We lost touch until she traced me after seeing my name in an ILO Directory. I believe that our meeting was not coincidental but part of God's divine plan. We had so much catching up to do and I was glad to learn that she was now married, had two children and was working in Geneva. We met frequently and we reminisced about our school days, the friends we had and our hobbies. During one of our chats, she mentioned that she knew a guy who would be good for me; she described him and when she revealed his name, it happened to be the same man that I had been spending time with. She told me that she knew him and could vouch for him, and that he would respect me and treat me well. I took it as a good sign and a confirmation that I was on the right track. I told her that we were doing some fun things, like going to the movies, watching plays, and trying different cuisines, and she was both surprised and delighted.

One evening, when I had gone out for dinner with him, I decided it was time to share my past of sexual abuse, the impact it had on me and how my faith in God had been instrumental for my healing. He listened attentively and after I finished, he told me that he was so sorry. He also shared his own past with me, which was something that made me appreciate him more. Allowing me into his world and opening up to me demonstrated that he liked me and trusted me.

As the weeks passed, I grew to like him even more because he did not put me under any pressure, in the sense that he didn't quickly declare that he had fallen in love and push for an intimate relationship. We allowed the friendship to evolve and I enjoyed being treated like a queen and I was very comfortable. One concern that would come up from time to time was on issues of faith. I wanted to understand and have insights on whether he was a practicing Christian because I wanted to ensure that we were walking in the same direction. So, even though he did not practice in the same way that I did, I sensed that he had a relationship with God. That was a source of assurance and made me feel at ease. I knew myself only too well: the minute that I had any discomfort, I would be ready to flee.

One evening after we had gone out for dinner and were exchanging text messages, as we often did to bid each other good night, he sent a message in which he confessed that he was in love with me. I got flustered because I knew that it was inevitable, given the time that we spent together but I had deliberately chosen not to address the likelihood of this happening because I knew what I was capable of doing.

In the past, when a good friendship was developing, once I saw signs of a guy falling in love, I would look for all the reasons why it could not work and start behaving in a way that would result in the relationship failing. I would be critical, cut the guy off brashly when he tried telling me how he felt and soon after the relationship would die a natural death. I did not want that to happen with this relationship, so I decided to ride on the wave of friendship and not think of 'what next?' It was when that moment came that I would cross that bridge, and when it did, my initial reaction was in how to respond to the message. Even though we had been open and honest with each other, I still had fears about exposing what I truly felt deep within me. My feeling was if I told him that I loved him, I would be opening the door to sexual intimacy. And once I did that, would a man love me or he would only be after sex? I was informed that sex was an expression of love between a couple but for me they were two separate issues. The question that was constantly in my mind was how could the man who sexually abused me have loved me? I knew that I had to work on my distorted perception of sex and love and I could not run away from it. I acknowledged his message and shied away from affirming my feelings. I didn't sleep much that night because I started pondering on what it meant, now that he had told me. I was excited that I was loved and also frightened that I also loved him. I truly believed that he did love me.

The following evening, I called up my Mom to seek wise counsel on how I could respond to this man's declaration of his love for me. She knew about the relationship and she was really excited for me because she detected my happiness and was encouraged that I had taken a great leap to cultivate a friendship with a man. She asked me a simple question, "Do you love him?" I told her that I thought I did and she then asked what the big deal was. We discussed it at length and she told me just to take one step at a time and not to start thinking of tomorrow and the future because we don't know what the future holds, and just enjoy each day. I thereafter chose to ride on the wave and enjoy what was at hand. I sent him a message and told him that I loved him too and he was delighted with the feedback. He told me that he would let me set the pace of the relationship. That was such an important statement because he knew my fears and struggles with relationships and was willing to set aside his own wants. It really touched me and I respected him more for that.

One of the highlights was a weekend trip that we took to see my Dad, who was once again Minister for Agriculture, since 2007, and was going to be in Rome to participate in a Food and Agriculture Organization meeting. I had not been back to Rome since 1988 and given that we had lived there before, I was longing to go back but I had not found the ideal moment. It was the right time so I shared my plans with my friend and asked him if he wanted to join me. He agreed and I was very surprised. He told me that he would be glad to meet my Dad and was honored to join me on this important trip since it was to retrace the paths of a place that had some great memories of my adolescent years. Again, I thought that this guy is really special, and so we went to Rome. I took him to John Cabot University where I had been a student for three years; to the neighborhood where we had first lived; to Via del Corso, where we shopped a little; past the Coliseum and of course, to meet Dad for dinner. It was good to see Dad and knowing him with his very forthright and blunt questions, such as 'What is your intention with my daughter and when are you going to marry her?' I prayed that he would not be too intimidating. Dad was cool and asked very general questions and later on, I heard from Mom that she had asked him not to frighten the man away since he was special to me. She also said that Dad liked my friend, who had made a good impression.

After spending a year together, I was relocated to Ethiopia and the distance didn't help. Much as we kept in touch and tried to meet, it was not as much as we would have wanted, and this strained the relationship. On top of that, he kept busy with work, maybe as a distraction since I was no longer there and I also was busy. We kept in regular touch and met after a couple of months but it was not practical and it was difficult to maintain the same flow in the relationship. Quite unexpectedly, a personal crisis on his part shook the relationship and after lengthy discussions over the phone, over email and face-to-face we agreed that it was best that we parted. Many times, I would reflect on the quote by Doug Horton that "If you love something let it go free. If it doesn't come back, you never had it. If it comes back, love it forever." We also discussed the fact that we were not tying ourselves to each other and if either one of us met someone else, we could move on. My friend who had recommended him to me and said that he was a good catch was saddened by the news of the break up. She couldn't understand but eventually came to terms with the news and accepted under the terms that if this was for the best, so be it.

This break up was painful but at the same time, I knew that we had parted not because we did not love each other but because circumstances were not conducive to our continuing. I consciously decided that I would not allow myself to feel bitterness, regrets, resentment, anger or those emotions that surface when relationships don't go as planned, and prayed to the Lord that He help me. God gave me strength and comforted me and I figured that this was not meant to be, at least during that season of my life. What I have learned from this experience is that life does not always go the way that we want or plan. Hence, I must choose how to deal with what the Lord allows to come my way. The relationship deserves mentioning because it was my first significant relationship since dealing with my abuse. The fact that this man had been patient, understanding and sensitive meant that I had learned to trust him. I now had the courage to do things that I had never done because I was fearful, even something so natural as holding his hand when I wanted to and telling him that I loved him. Inviting him to meet my Dad was the right thing to do, and I wanted Dad to see and meet a man who had been good to me. Little did I know that this would be the one and only special man in my life whom I would get an opportunity to introduce to him. I am so grateful to God for the chance that He availed for Dad to meet the one man who had taken my hand and walked with me on a journey of self-discovery in the context of a man-woman relationship.

From time to time I keep in touch with this man but I am not waiting with baited breath for us to get back together. Why do I say that? No promises were made by either one us. However, I have not yet met someone with whom I am ready to share my life. The doors are open, though, and if it is part of God's master plan, we will get together, but if not I accept that it is not God's desire for us and He knows why. Should that be the case then I accept that God has another plan, which has got to be better for both of us. And who am I to question God?

In the meantime, I have reached an interesting point where I am at peace with where I am emotionally. I am not bitter or desperate and avoid complaining about not yet having settled down with a loving mate. I am sure those of you who are also single can relate with this. My sisters, allow me to advise you to let those yearning feelings go. They are poison to your body... I will not deny the fact that loneliness does strike me from time to time and I begin to wish that I could meet someone with whom I'd want to share my life. What options do I have? I could go out and look for a likely candidate but frankly, I don't have energy for that and on top of that, where would I start? This could be a topic for another book, so let's just say that I have decided not to fret and rather, I keep myself occupied and refuse to lament on what I do not have. It's so easy to compare myself with others and wonder what I must not be doing right, to feel guilty and entertain pity parties. The truth is, I am so cool with being single because what I know for certain is that I will not go out looking for a man. I have been there before, in search of a man. Many of us have been there and you can attest to the fact that sometimes what you fished out ended up being a disaster...

I believe that even now some of my relatives have just given up any hope of me ever getting married. Since leaving Lesotho in 1999, I go home for holidays every year, and each time I have been asked the same question, over and over again "So, Hopo where is the husband? We really want to eat your wedding cake!" I got so tired of this question that about four years ago, I told my Mom that next time they asked, I was going to say "You know what? I don't want to get married!" and that should stop the questions. So, when I went on the next holiday, the same question arose and this time I was ready with my response. I told them that I did not want to get married. You should have seen the shock on their faces; they were left speechless and sure enough, that put a stop to any marriage-related questions.

I know that I shall get married. I have unshakeable faith that God is in control, that He has not forgotten me and marriage shall surely come to pass. I know that those that put their trust in the Lord cannot be put to shame. I know that it's not about my desires or schedule but His perfect timing and I trust the Lord, who knows what is best for me and knows to work things out for me. I do not want to be in a relationship which will give me grief and sorrow. I have seen too many of those and I really believe it is better to be single and content rather than to be married and miserable.

Having faith in God is fundamental and a core value for any relationship that I might entertain. On anything else I am willing to compromise but not on matters of faith. The Lord is at the centre of my life and I cannot imagine waking up and finding myself with someone who does not agree with me on the fundamentals of faith. My friends know me, and though we might not agree when it comes to this discussion they have let it go because they know that I am not budging. The Lord took me out of a tough situation and during those bleak days, when I had nobody else to turn to, I had Him to call upon and so if I turn my back on Him, where can I go? I'd be lost without Him. My prayer is that the Lord will help me to remain faithful because even those standing resolute in their faith have been shaken and sidelined.

At this time my eyes are focused on what the Lord can do and I am standing firm with Him. I have seen couples with different faiths content in their relationships and I have seen others of different faiths who are miserable and frustrated. I believe that in matters of the heart each one has a story to tell and each one must follow their heart...

I am looking for particular traits in a man, but I have been told that my standards are too high. I know that they are because I am going by God's standards. My late Dad also could not understand what I was looking for and one of his prayers was that he not die before I got married. Like any parent, it was natural that he would want to see all his children settled before he parted from this earth. Pops had been blessed to be married to Mom for 46 years, and as such he had experienced the joy of sharing his life with someone he loved and respected. Having witnessed their love mature over the years and how Mom was there for him until the very end of his journey is of course, something that I admire and also want to experience.

While I was in Addis my parents visited me, Pops more times than Mom since his job as the Minister for Agriculture entailed his participation in several meetings. Out of Bole airport in Addis you can fly to anyplace in the world, so he usually stopped by on his way to West Africa and we had those precious father and daughter moments, which now that he is gone, I treasure more than ever. It's so important to honor and respect our parents, after all that they did to shape us to be the people we are. The least we can do is to bless them and appreciate them while they are with us and not once they have departed. Buying the most expensive coffin and holding a funeral that turns heads is not worth the money or effort if while they were alive you were not able to spend time with them and tell them how much they meant to you. To put on a show once they have departed is futile. The time to do all those things is now, while they are still alive. There might be some of you who are estranged from your parents and have not been able to have a good relationship with them. Maybe you are not even on talking terms. My advice is make peace with them. Put your pride aside and take that first step, ask for forgiveness and really mean it and begin to work on that relationship. I agree that it may not be easy but prayer can change things, so don't forget to add in a big dose of prayer and things will work out.

The loss of my Dad was a big blow. It impressed upon me the fact that we are just passing through this earth, hence we need to make the most of every day. My dad celebrated his 75th birthday on 26 July 2009 and a month and one day later, he passed on. He had always told us that his 75th birthday was a milestone and he wanted to celebrate it with his children, their spouses and grandchildren. We were planning to make it a birthday to remember but little did we know that it would not materialize. Three months before his birthday, he told my mom that he wanted to see all his children in Bristol, where my sister and family live. So, in early July, my brother, my sister and Mom and I congregated in Bristol to be with Pops and it was then that we learned that he was in the terminal stages of cancer. As we spent time with him it reminded us of days past when we were much younger and the family was just the three children and the parents. We were now adults and God had been so good to us. Luckily, on his last birthday, we had a subdued gathering with his grandchildren (my sister's children), his son-in-law, his son, his daughters and his spouse. My brothers' family could not come, so even though that was unfortunate, he got more or less what he had desired.

For the three weeks that I spent with Dad, on the days when he was up to it, he would call us for family conferences and he would discuss the estate, the future of his pet project, a newspaper 'The Monitor', that he founded and that had wide readership in Lesotho, our individual plans for the future and the wellbeing of Mom. He would give us his perspectives and his advice, always reminding us that we would be responsible for the decisions that we took. One of the most difficult things for me was to see his witty and sharp mind actively at work but his body was just no longer cooperating with him. I think that it must have been a source of frustration for him, given that this was a man who had run marathons, owned a farm and was involved in cultivation of a variety of crops, encouraged and motivated farmers to cultivate their fields, injected and cured animals of all kinds and involved in supervising the construction of his homes. On some days he would be quiet, reflective and not wanting to be disturbed and we would respect that and give him the space that he wanted.

Other days, he would ask to see each one of us individually and have one-to-one talks with us. I remember one particular conversation we had, which was so painful. He told me his concern and how sad he was that he had not seen me married. He said after I had been abused, and now that I had overcome, marriage would complete the circle of me having moved on. That not being the case, he prayed that one day I would meet that man who would afford me the opportunity to experience a good marriage.

Some mornings, I would wake up feeling so sad and helpless and I did not know what to do. Each one in the family had a task

– on alternate nights and days, Mom and my brother would nurse Pops and my sister, upon her return from work would also chip in and nurse Dad. No one told me explicitly that I could not nurse Dad but when I offered they would tell me that there was no need because everything was under control. Instead they proposed that since they enjoyed my good cooking (which I do when I have the time), I could do the cooking and washing up dishes. Months after Pops passed on I asked Mom, why they didn't want me to nurse Pops and she told me that Pops said that I had already gone through much pain when I was abused and he did not want me to go through anymore pain. He wanted to protect me from me seeing his pain. That was such a loving gesture that Mom and my siblings respected. Maybe, Pops better than anyone else at that point could relate to the fact that when I was going through the pain of abuse, he felt so helpless and so now, as he was going through pain, he knew how helpless I felt and so it was better to shield me...

There were days when Mom or my brother had not gotten enough sleep and were tired and depressed and then a wave of sadness would hit all of us. I would detect it and I knew from my past, that when such waves come, you have to nip them in the bud. I would muster all the strength that I had and gather us together in prayer and ask the Lord to give us strength. God would restore our joy and remind us of the hilarious things that Pops would say and do, which would lighten the mood and lift our spirits. I had learned in dealing with sexual abuse that it is so important to look for the pleasant and positive events in our lives and to dwell on them.

There were other days when reality hit us that Pops would soon no more be with us, unless the Lord performed a miracle in which he would be totally cured of cancer. At the same time, we knew that we could not bank on this happening because that was the Lord's prerogative. However, if we paused and looked around us, miracles were happening. The doctor who was assigned to Dad really connected with him and that made a big difference in his demeanor. She later on mentioned that her speciality was dealing with terminal patients, so we thanked God for bringing her our way.

We would ask ourselves how the relatives would take the news that Dad wanted to be cremated. Cremation is not a common practice in Lesotho and it is expected that people view the deceased before burial in order to bring closure. This was something that they would be denied and it was beyond our control. We decided that we would cross that bridge when we got there and for now, it was important to assure Dad that his wishes would be respected.

Even though this was a taxing period for all of us, we never had any arguments or were irritable with each other; instead we grew closer and when one of us sensed that a hug or a prayer was needed, we would be quick to offer it. When tears flowed, we would encourage each other to cry. Tears are good and allowed us to release our pain. My sister's family was also a pillar of strength – they would allow my sister to be with us full time, rather than being at home, and her husband and sons would offer to run errands and the grandchildren would come in and check on their granddad. For those of you who have lost a family member unexpectedly, you know what it means when you cannot say your goodbye but we were very fortunate to have had time with Dad and to bid him farewell and for him to be able to tell us his last wishes. My Dad planned his memorial service and it was then up to us to execute it as he had requested.

I had a wonderful relationship with my Dad, and I cherish the time that I had with him. After he knew of the sexual abuse he became protective of me and he wanted to shield his baby daughter from anything that could cause me pain. The morning when I saw him for the last time, my eyes were filled with tears and I tried to be strong while he looked at me with so much love and did not say a word. I said, "Pops, if I don't see you again, I hope to see you on the other side," and I left without looking back. And I went straight into Mom's arms to shed the burden of my tears.

Then I took one of the longest trips that I have ever taken - from Bristol to Dar. This trip was long because of the sad thoughts, knowing that I would no longer see Dad. I was just about to lose someone very significant in my life and it was difficult to come to terms with that. Also, I did not have a network of friends in Dar and a church family since I had decided to move out of the place where I had been going for five months. If I had such a church family, I could count on people calling me, praying with me and just taking time to ask me how I was doing. Since this was not the case, I knew that I would be on my own and missed being with Mom and my sister, as they went through the final leg of the journey with Pops. I would only be told about his very last days and not witness it for myself. I eventually made peace with the fact that God wanted to spare my brother and me from that (my brother had left few days before me to go back to work and to his family in the US).

One of the first things that I did upon my return from Bristol to Dar was to make time to say goodbye to Pops. He was not yet gone but I sensed it that it was a matter of time and I had too many emotions that I had to release. How I did this was by writing. I wrote Pops a goodbye letter as I reflected on the privilege of having known what it was to have a father who cared and loved me. I remembered the hilarious moments, the trips that we had taken over the years, the fun things we had done, the disagreements and the squabbles that we had had. I also remembered one day when he had come home from work and told me that I needed to forgive him because he had done something terrible. I asked him why I needed to forgive him and he told me that he had been in a meeting of high government officials and had told them that his daughter had been sexually abused as a child and not told a soul and how it had been so damaging. I asked him to tell me more about the context of the meeting. He said that there was a report tabled where a complaint had been filed by a woman who was being sexually harassed and his male colleagues wanted to push the issue under the carpet on the basis that there was no evidence to prove that it had happened. My Dad said that he got mad and he started to think of the damaging effects that it would have on the woman, who would have to carry her pain and suffering in silence for the rest of her life. He remembered how I had remained silent over the years and so he decided to take a stand for this woman. That was how he got pulled into the discussion and as a result, a decision was taken for the man who had been sexually harassing the woman to be punished. I was so proud of Dad and I told him that he had done the right thing and there was no need for forgiveness. I told him if any situations arose, he must be free to share my story and speak out for the woman or man whose rights had been infringed. Writing the letter was very therapeutic and gave me a sense of peace.

I plunged into work as a distraction from dwelling on what it meant to lose a loved one and reflecting on my relationship with Dad. My sister and mom faithfully called me every evening to let me know how Dad was doing. I left Bristol, three weeks before he passed on and with each passing day he rapidly deteriorated. I spoke to him only once and it was just a few words because he tired quickly and was on pain medication that made him drowsy. My mom and sister don't know what those calls meant but they were so important as they were my only connection with them and Pops and prevented me from sinking into an abyss of solitude and regret over my inability to help him. I'll never forget the day, 27 August 2009 when my sister called me and told me that Pops had passed on. It was no surprise because I already knew somehow, but I was numb and empty, knowing that it was now real that I would never see him again on this earth.

Pops had requested, for the day of his memorial, that only people who knew him say a few words, including my brother and I. He detested funerals where people who had barely known the deceased would speak a lot of empty words. He had made it clear that this would not be the case for him. Having served as a Minister of Agriculture and being a man that loved his country with a passion that I had never seen in anyone else, it was no surprise that the memorial was well attended.

That day the sky was blue with a sprinkling of clouds and the sun shone brightly, a perfect day to say goodbye to a man I loved and respected. The ceremony went smoothly and all too soon, it was my turn to speak, and what do you say when you have dignitaries such as His Majesty, King Letsie III and the Honorable Deputy Prime Minister, Archibald Lesao Lehohla in the audience? I had spent time asking God to give me a message that would touch people. We had also prayed that this day would be a celebration of a life well spent, as we bid our farewell. I lifted my eyes to heaven and drew strength from the Lord to speak as He would guide me. I forgot about myself and filled with emotions that I barely managed to contain, spoke about a man who had been my loving Dad for some forty-odd years. I explained that if I had the choice to choose a father, I would choose him again. People who spoke on that day also spoke about a man they respected, appreciated and loved. In his message, the Deputy Prime Minister spoke words that I will always remember. He drew from the poem, 'The Ladder of Saint Augustine' by Henry Wadsworth Longfellow: "The heights by great men reached and kept were not attained by sudden flight but they, while their companions slept were toiling upward in the night," and informed the august audience that his own Dad had spoken these words to him and his brother. He said that these words described what Dad represented. At the end of the day, we were at peace, confidently knowing that that Pop's memorial had gone as he had wanted and that we had bid farewell to a true hero.

The process of putting the pieces together after the loss of Dad is another gradual journey, like climbing Mount Kilimanjaro, but I can attest to the fact that time heals and every day is better than the last. The memories live on and I do miss Pops. When I need advice or guidance on important decisions regarding work or a financial investment, I am tempted to send him an email or to give him a call; then I remember that this is not an option any longer. The tears come from time to time and that is expected. When I talk to Mom and my siblings there are past moments that can we laugh about as we remember him with love. Friends have been instrumental in sending emails and calling me to share the burden of my loss, especially those who also knew Pops.

Pop's passing on impressed upon me that we get only one, not two, nor three chances to pass through this earth and that we are all going to pass on and no one is here indefinitely. Then I ask myself why we live as though we are here forever. How many of us can truly say that when that times comes, we will be ready to depart? How many of us have unresolved issues that we refuse to deal with because we believe that we still have time? Let's not kid ourselves because no one can say for sure when his time will come. How do we spend our days? Do we spend each day of our lives working like crazy yet have no time for loved ones? Or do we spend our lives searching for meaning in the things that we do but we cannot find it? And then we resolve that as long as we are doing anything, it's acceptable?

I believe that it is important we ask ourselves why we do what we do and what is the reason for us to be alive. Once we begin to answer these questions, my hope is that we can see beyond the jobs that that we do and discover our life purposes. When we come to the end of our life's journey, it will be great to leave a legacy, not of the material assets that we accumulated but of the seeds that we sowed and invested in someone's life. Whatever we accumulated is of no use because it cannot define who we were and we leave it all behind anyway.

It is the lives that we influenced, and are remembered for having made a difference in, are what remains forever. Ultimately I believe that having the Lord in our lives is what gives meaning and purpose to our lives.

VIII

On countless instances, I still cannot believe that it is I who went through the traumatic experience of sexual abuse. I look at the life I lead now and it is so different from the days when I struggled with my dark ordeal. I have found peace and meaning in what I went through and the story does not end there. God has been so good to me. I live a life of gratitude and each day is filled with lessons that I learn through the challenges that I overcome. These make me the better person that I daily become. I just cannot stop thanking God for bringing me thus far and I really do believe that without Him, I would not be who I am. In fact, I often wonder what would have become of me if I had not come to His saving grace.

I am convinced that out of the deep hurts and sufferings that we have endured, our greatest ministries are birthed. And as we journey through this life, we might not have the complete picture but with each passing day, if we search hard enough, we can begin to see the pieces of the jigsaw puzzle come together. I write to the young women who have gone through even worse situations than my own and I say, there is hope and not all is lost... The Word of God says in Isaiah 43, verse 2 that "When you pass through the waters, I will be with you; when you pass through the rivers, they will not sweep over you; when you walk through the fire, you will not be burned; the flames will not set you ablaze." The verses do not say "If" but it says "When", so we will go through tough situations and there is no way of avoiding them.

Climbing Mount Kilimanjaro was a significant milestone. It was one of those things that I would never have imagined doing. How could I go on my own and do something that so few did? I never believed that I had the courage and the determination to do something so daring. For so many years, I had done a good job at putting myself down and not believing in myself. Climbing Kili was a test, to prove to myself that I could do the unimaginable, if I dispelled all of my fears and took a great leap of faith. I was determined to change my language from 'I cannot' to 'I can' and believed that once I had conquered Kili I would be ready to take up other challenges. I am not yet where I want to be but I am a work in progress. It's *'pole, pole'*, which means 'slowly, slowly', which was what my guide kept reminding me as I climbed Kili.

So, unlike many climbers, who plan for a lifetime to climb Kili, for me the decision to climb was made quickly, almost at the spur of the moment. Had it not been this way, I might have talked myself out of doing it. Many things I plan to do but climbing Mount Kili certainly was not one of them; hence, this was very unlike Hops. How was this idea birthed? I had come to Dar es Salaam while I was working in Addis to participate in a one week workshop and I was staying at the Kempinski Hotel. Hanging on the wall in my room was a picture of Kili and as I stood there admiring the picture I thought to myself that people actually climbed this mountain. I wondered what it would be like if I climbed it, but then I dismissed the thought. I looked at the picture again and noted the ruggedness and bareness of the mountain and I liked the idea of the challenge and thought that it might be a great idea... I didn't give climbing another thought but when I looked at the picture during the rest of my stay, it was as if Mount Kili was luring me.

When I left Dar after the workshop, I did not entertain any more thoughts of climbing Kili and thought that it had been a far-fetched idea. Later that year when I started planning for my annual vacation in August, I decided that I would go visit a dear friend in Trinidad and Tobago. I started communicating with my friend and she informed me that August was not the best time to visit since it was the rainy season in that part of the world. The thought of just looking at the beach but being unable to enjoy it didn't sound like a good idea, let alone the money that I would have to spend to get there just to be besieged by the rain- it turned out that this plan was not a good idea. We agreed that it would have to be some other time. However, I was at a loss concerning what to do to substitute that plan. Then, it dawned on me to climb Kili and the idea resonated deeply. I decided to pray about it and the more I did, the more I got excited and thought 'Yeah that sounds cool!' Immediately, I made contact with a very good friend of mine- she had climbed Kili two years before- and she excitedly told me what I needed and which travel agent to contact. I immediately contacted the travel agent, who sent me information on the climb and what it entailed, and thereafter I made the necessary bookings. I decided that after climbing Mount Kilimanjaro, I would need some pampering so I thought a hotel with a spa by the beach would be an ideal place to go. My mind started wondering and I imagined how lovely it would be, after six days climbing the mountain without any luxuries, to be lounging on a beach chair under an umbrella, reading a good book and in the background hearing the receding waves. And any time I wanted, I could take a stroll along the pristine white beaches and then I would slowly wade into the warm and blue ocean until I could start swimming.

Having been a runner for several years, I was rather confident that I could manage the climb but my friend warned me that while being fit is important, how well you acclimatize is even more critical. One might be a marathon runner but if one does not acclimatize, one will probably not reach the summit. Short cuts are not recommended and it is critical that climbers acclimatize; this was one thing that I learned when I climbed the highest peak in Africa (5985 metres) - and the tallest free-standing mountain in the world. The journey ends up being a long one because rather than simply going up, it's a gradual climb in which you ascend to a certain level and then climb down a short distance for the night and then begin to climb further the next day. When I was preparing for Mount Kilimanjaro one of the things that my friend also warned me against was not to take any short cuts with the gear needed. She proposed that I purchase a good wind breaker, thermal T-shirts, the right hiking shoes, gloves and sweatshirts.

Weeks before I climbed Kili, I started to draw up my supply lists and since I was going to be in Geneva before my climb, I knew that I could buy all the necessary paraphernalia. I managed to get all the supplies but forgot to purchase an air mattress, which would have been a fantastic idea. I remember telling my Mom and Dad that I was going to climb Kili and I expected them to be excited but it was like 'Go for it!' When I told my friends that I was going to climb Kili, I got mixed reactions ranging from "Are you sure that you want to go spend your holiday straining your muscles?" to "Wow, go for it girl, you're something!" After getting these kinds of remarks, I decided that there was no need to make much noise about my plan to climb Kili. After all, I didn't want to get discouraged before I even started climbing. Maybe climbing Kili was just no big deal, especially for Africans, who would rather opt for going to other places where they could shop. I guess if I had said that I was going to Dubai, Bangkok or New York, I would have received a different reaction.

August came and with excited nerves I boarded the plane for my one hour flight to Kilimanjaro International Airport. When I arrived at the airport, someone was supposed to pick me up but with a name like Hopolang Phororo, I have learned that people don't know who to expect. When I left the luggage pick-up no placards were uplifted bearing my name and I was getting rather concerned, so I asked one of the men lingering around if someone from Keys Hotel was around and he told me to wait because surely someone would come, as if that was useful advice! Finally, a man sheepishly approached me and brought out a very tired-looking piece of paper with my name totally mutilated. He politely tried to hide his shock and surprise when I made myself known to him. After we had gotten into the car, I could not resist and I asked him why he was so surprised and he told me that he was not expecting a woman of colour but a Caucasian. And I was tempted to add a man, at that! I learned that women of colour, particularly daughters from the continent were a rare species on Kili and so this was quite an honor and reiterated my point that I was doing something out of the ordinary. During my ascent I was beset by unending questions of where I came from and countless marriage proposals from the guides and porters, who were so delighted and proud of me.

As we drove to Moshi, I kept trying to get a glimpse of Mount Kili and finally, I saw her in her majesty, towering above all peaks in Africa and luring me to test the vagaries of her terrain. I wanted to get a closer look at what I was up against, but large clouds billowing obscured her; she was like a shy schoolgirl who does not want to reveal too much, and I could barely get a good peek. I guess the full magnitude of what it takes to climb Kili can only be experienced when one starts the climb. One is not sure what to expect until one starts climbing Mount Kili. Even before we climb Kili, we could also ask those who have climbed what to expect and they could give us guidance. However, climbing Mount Kili is a personal journey and its only in climbing it that we can truly know what lies ahead for each one of us. It's just like our lives: people can tell us what to expect but no one's journey through life can ever be the same as another's, and we can never know what to expect in life. We just have to start living it out. However, if we could know what lies ahead of us, life would be so much easier. We deceive ourselves by thinking we are living our lives by faith because when troubling seasons come we don't trust in God, and we justify our lack of faith that surely, there is no harm in getting some insights from outside sources. We confidently visit fortune tellers hoping that as they read our palms, look into the magic balls and you name it, they will be able to give us the full picture. Granted they might give us a glimpse of what is to come but even that takes the excitement out of living.

I believe strongly that if God wanted to unravel the big picture of what we can expect in our journey through life He could but if He did that there would be no reason for us to live by faith. Needless to say, sometimes, I do wish that He would show me certain parts of my life but then He is God and I thank Him that He does not. I sit back and start to practice and flex my faith muscles and hold on to His promises that He is in control and nothing that I go through in this journey of life is wasted.

Conquering Kili is not an overnight journey. It is gradual and requires careful preparation, great perseverance and focus. It is not a journey in which you compete with others but it is a personal journey with well-defined milestones. You go steadily and at your own pace. For six days, each morning, I would leave the camp sites with my guide at 08h00 and get to the next site at around 15h00. The route that I opted for was the Machame route, which was said to be the most scenic but also one of the more rugged and challenging routes. Each day, we were going higher and higher and the landscape changed progressively. We started from Machame Gate then went to Machame Camp (2 890 m), then on to Shira Camp (3 840 m), next up to Lava Tower Camp (4 630 m) but back down to Barranco Camp (3 950 m), then up to Barafu Camp (4 550 m), then to Stella Point (5 756 m) and finally, to Uhuru Peak (5 895 m).

Other climbers who were also determined to reach Uhuru peak would arrive at the camp sites earlier and others would arrive later. Each person set their own pace; it was not a race, the goal being to reach the summit and it would take the willpower of each to keep going. Even in our lives, we set milestones and once we have reached them, we move to the next level. Moving up in my career in the ILO has been like climbing Mount Kili since it has entailed a gradual progression. For each person it differs.

Some move up the ladder very fast and others move up very slowly. Some people move up quickly because of their extensive networks and who they are connected to; others move up because someone recognizes their hard work and perseverance. Others move up slowly because their efforts are not recognized, while others might have given up but live in the hope that something might change and one day they will be promoted, and others might still be assessing their options as to how they want to progress.

Moving to where I am in the organization has required a season of learning several lessons that have prepared me for where I am today. For instance, it has taken me great perseverance and focus to still be a part of the organization that I work for. Talking of focus brings me back to Kili, where one has got to be focused and determined to reach the top. Unfocused people and those who easily give up cannot reach Uhuru Peak. Climbing Kili is not for the fainthearted. One must be content to go through some hard patches when things don't go as planned. The consolation is always that nothing is permanent and all things must come to pass. Sleeping in a tent on a thin mattress and hard floor every night and being deprived of the luxuries and amenities was not easy. After few days, my hips were sore and I was not quite sure how to sleep but once I got accustomed to the pain, I no longer felt it and life went on. Sometimes to make progress, one has to forfeit the pleasures of the present to reap greater benefits in the future.

The last day of climbing Kili was the most difficult part of the journey. We left base at midnight and climbed in the scree for six hours. It was one step forward and two steps backwards. As I climbed and looked up, I could see the head torches of those ahead of me, climbing higher and higher but never quite reaching the top. I got so discouraged and began to wonder what on earth I was doing at that time of the night on Mount Kili when I should be in my bed. I despaired and asked myself, "When will I ever reach the top?" My guide picked up my discouragement and advised me not to look up but to look down at my feet and to take a step at a time. Having conquered Kili afforded me a special relationship that I forged and which remains close to me, as a journey of self-reflection. I learned from this tough experience that sometimes the last leg before reaching a goal is the most difficult and that is when we are ready to give up. I can relate this to when things just did not seem to be working for me to get settled in my job, and the natural inclination was to compare myself with other colleagues, who seemed to be settled and making progress. I wondered why I could not be like them but I forgot that it was just my own perspective. Maybe if I asked them, I would find out that I was actually better off in the situation that I was in. That quickly stopped all comparisons and I regained focus. I reminded myself that this was the path that I had to walk alone and it was not like so and so's. And I knew that just when the breakthrough is eminent, that is the time when you are ready to throw in the towel and give up. But that is the time to hold on, so I decided to keep on keeping on and the result was that, not only did I finally reach Uhuru Peak but I also found my place in the ILO, where I could make a difference. It was exhilarating to get to the peak, a place I wanted to reach to see what it was about, to discover why so many others traveled great distances to reach it. It felt good to be counted among the many climbers who had conquered Kili. However, for me it was not so much reaching Uhuru peak that had changed me but the journey up Mount Kilimanjaro. So, even in the same vein, it is not that I have arrived at the ultimate pinnacle of success in the ILO; I will have to be the Director General for that to be true, but it's all the accumulated experiences of being in the different positions that I have held before that have been critical to me for my position as the Deputy Director.

There are a number of crucial lessons that I have taught and continue to teach to my Daughters of Destiny, who I had been involved with since 2003, in Namibia, as you'll recall in Chapter 5. However, when I left Windhoek, I believed that as God had given me the opportunity to work and live in different countries, it was not by coincidence and I could make my contribution by mentoring young women wherever I happened to find myself. I believed that if I could make a difference even in the life of just one young woman, it was good enough. However, I still had to figure out what form and shape the Daughters would take. In Windhoek, Daughters was an established group, so I could not just emulate it but I had to find a critical mass of young women who saw a need and wanted to be a part of such a Ministry, and then adapt it to the country context. This initial groundwork needed me to be in a place for more than a few months, which did not happen when I was in Abidjan and Addis since I was in each of the places for less than a year. In addition, there were just too many other things happening in my life, so the last thing on my mind was starting Daughters of Destiny.

Within a few months of arriving in Geneva I did not waste time and started exploring how I could start a group. One of my prospective members was a young African woman I met in a youth employment meeting at the ILO. She was doing an internship. We started talking and among other issues, I learned that she was a Christian. We then agreed to meet for coffee. As I got to know her better, I shared with her my idea to organize a group for young women. She was all in support of it and believed that it was also a good place for her to make new friends. Church was another place where I met several young women. A youth ministry was in place but it seemed to cater to all youth, even though they were a heterogeneous group with very different needs. Having being a youth leader when I was living in Lesotho, I knew that during youth meetings, it was difficult to address the specific needs of everyone, so the tendency was to focus more on the spiritual rather than on the person's other needs. I saw a rich field to harvest members for the Daughters and prayed for guidance.

One day, I was talking to one of the young women and she said how she wished that there was a group for young women in the church because the youth ministry was not for her. She explained that for young women above 18 years old, it was not easy to relate to the young people who were under 18 years old. I believed that this was an answer to my prayer. I shared with her my vision to start a group and she welcomed it. I started meeting her regularly just as I did with the other young woman I had met in the ILO in order to know each one of them better, to understand their fears, their dreams and also to share my story with them. Knowing that I was going to leave Geneva at some point, I thought that these two young women could become the champions for Daughters of Destiny. Months later, I invited both of the two young women to my place and I told them what I saw as their leadership roles in Daughters. One of them was rather hesitant and felt that she could not manage such a responsibility, while the other one was rearing to go.

These two young women took an instant liking to each other and we had an amazing meeting. I was very open and honest with them as I shared with them what sexual abuse had done to me and the challenges that I struggled with, including relationships, self-confidence and self-esteem. I was consciously creating an environment where they too would feel free and safe to open up. I had learned that when you want people to talk, it's important to open up and allow yourself to become vulnerable. As they see that you are genuine and real, they can relate and begin to open up. The young women opened up and shared their own struggles. We then prayed together and spoke a little about the Daughters. We had these kinds of meetings for about three months until we felt comfortable to cast the net wider and bring in other girls. Much as they were very excited about the bigger group, they wanted my assurance that they could still continue to meet me individually and together. I allayed their fears that we could do so.

I shared my vision for the Daughters with the Pastor of the church and we agreed that we would portray the group as a separate entity from the church, to avoid the notion that it was church based and catered to just Christians. Even though the foundation was on Christian values, since this was what I could relate to, we welcomed any young woman to be a part of the group. We drew up some ideas of what we could do with the young women and the two young women invited others. Most of the young women were in their twenties. A colleague at work helped me to get a venue for the meetings, given that with my limited French I might have failed to convey a clear message. We met in a community centre that was well situated and paid a nominal fee for our meetings, which took place two Saturdays a month.

Activities and events revolved around discussions of issues that they struggled with as young women and this included relationships, dating, dressing and grooming, attitudes, low self-confidence and self-esteem. We would also hang out together at picnics, dinners, celebrate birthdays and go to Christian concerts. In this way, the girls were also building friendships among themselves, which to this day are still going strong. As they each had an opportunity to take the lead in some of these activities, their confidence levels were boosted. A month before I left Geneva, we decided to hold a launch of the Daughters in the hope of increasing our membership. The young women took charge and planned the event at a hotel in the centre of town. The event included singing, dancing, sharing their testimonies on what the Daughters group had done for them, as well as sharing the vision of the group. There were about twenty people who participated. I was so touched later that night, when the mother of one of the Daughters came up to me with tears in her eyes and said how she was so grateful for the Daughters. She said that she was so shocked to see her daughter, who she always known as so shy, to be dancing with so much confidence before an audience. The launch stirred some interest but once I left Geneva, the meetings became infrequent. One of the champions tried to sustain the momentum because she believed in the vision but she could not do it on her own. With time, the young women went their different ways; some got married and others went on to further their studies; however, they continue to communicate with each other and from time they visit with one another.

It was an enriching experience to have been the founder of the Daughters in Geneva. I felt that I had met a need as a big sister to the young African women. Many of them had spent some years in Geneva and other parts of Europe and had to grapple with issues of finding their own identities in schools and workplaces in the midst of peer pressure. In order to sometimes be accepted, they would have to dress, talk and behave in a certain way. I felt that one of my responsibilities was to impress upon them that they had to be content as they were and did not need to change in order to fit in with the crowds.

When I got to Addis, I decided to go with the same approach even though I was concerned that when the time came for me to leave, the same situation as had happened would prevail. I decided that would not hinder me and that would be dealt with as time progressed. Addis was even more complicated because I did a lot of traveling, so keeping a regular schedule of meetings with the young women was not possible. I met a group of young women at church and as I got talking to them about the Daughters, they seemed excited about forming a group. I also spoke to the Pastor and informed him about the vision and he was in support of it. I told him that we would initially meet in my house and then with time we would have to find a public place to meet. I started the group with four young women. The first meeting was just to get to know each other better and to share the vision of Daughters and describe the group in Geneva. I could not share the vision of Daughters without delving into my past of sexual abuse. The girls were generally a little younger than the ones in Geneva, and they were totally shocked at what had happened and did not know what to say. I encouraged them to ask me any question that they had since I had gone through a healing phase and I was ready to share.

Even though they told me about themselves, I sensed that they were not ready to totally open up. Maybe they didn't know how and they were not ready to do it in the presence of the other girls. I did not push and so we kept to topics that they were most comfortable with. We met at my house for about three months and then the group started getting larger. I decided that it was better for us to move to a public place since when they came to my house, the young women would see how I lived and I wanted to avoid a situation where I would be asked to give them this or that. We started meeting at a coffee shop and met twice a month, or as my schedule permitted. The young women invited their friends from the university, from school and I invited an intern from the office. Most of them were in their late teens and early twenties and included few Nigerians, but most were Ethiopians.

We would meet in public places, discuss relevant topics, similar to the ones we had discussed in the Daughters in Geneva, go out for meals together, and watch movies. One challenge that we had was that most of the girls only spoke Amharic, so we had to make sure that in our midst, we had an interpreter. When there was no-one to interpret, communication was a real challenge. We had at least four girls who were staying at an orphanage, and who consistently participated in the meetings and they would contribute to the discussions. During every meeting, I insisted that all the girls should air their views. It was important for them to overcome the fear of public speaking. We had some very vocal girls in our sessions but with time, they also learned the importance of allowing others to talk and listening to their viewpoints. I remember one of the Ethiopian girls told me that I was one of her African role models because even though I was not an Ethiopian, I shared my resources, time and experiences with them. Those kinds of messages really inspired and motivated me to persevere. I told her that my passion was to share with them my experiences and to motivate them because I believed that they could become successful women. As I continued to meet with the girls, I could sense the ones who needed one-to-one meetings and I would arrange to meet up with them. I would ask questions, they would respond and begin to open up. However, I could only meet so many of them and wished that I had other women who could share the burden of mentoring young women.

I grew very close to the young women and they saw me as a big sister, as the Geneva young women had done. One of the champions from Geneva came on a work-related trip to Addis and I invited her to come and share about the Daughters. She testified about what her being a member of the Daughters in Geneva had meant and how it changed her life. Her message was well received and the young women understood that it was up to them to take hold of what they could get out of the Daughters or miss out on an opportunity to start believing that they could become something, no matter how humble their beginnings were. In addition, the Ethiopian Daughters could begin to see that they were a part of a bigger vision.

When the time came for me to leave Addis for Dar es Salaam, the girls were saddened by the news and once again, I was unsure whether the girls would continue to meet. There were two of the Daughters who believed in the vision and were eager to continue with the meetings. They managed for a while and then, like the Geneva group, the girls moved on, some to join the world of work and others continued with further studies. However, when I go to Addis for work related trips, I meet the Daughters that are still there.

It used to bother me that the group disbanded when I left and I asked myself whether I was the link that brought the young women together, and figured that I was. However, as I reflected further, I realized that given where these women were in the life cycle, they move on and so, for that season, when I am available for them, it's wonderful to have invested some pearls of wisdom in their lives that will make them better women. The groups would only be sustained if the young women themselves were roping in new members and planning for meetings and activities. Nevertheless, given that they too might feel that they have not yet acquired much experience and they have to work out their own lives, they feel inadequate to assume such a big burden. It is only women like myself, who, having reached a certain stage in our lives and are passionate about seeing young women grow, can make time for them and sustain the groups.

Addis was a significant place for the Daughters of Destiny Ministry because this was where we came up with a logo for the Daughters. We had a competition, for which I requested the girls to draw a logo that would go with the motto "Giving to receive'. The motto was symbolic of the fact that each of the young women who participated actively had received something, whether it was their confidence or self-esteem that had been boosted; they had learned something new or they had acquired improved communication or listening skills, and therefore I expected them to go and also touch the life of a younger girl in their own lives. I received many proposals and together with the young women at the last meeting of the Daughters we selected the logo. It was a combination of different logos – five small candles receiving light from one big candle.

My next duty station was Dar and it took me some time to start a Daughters group. Work kept me busy most of the time and I was also wondering whether a different approach could work. I prayed about it and I thought about starting a mentorship programme. I had been involved in a similar programme in Windhoek, so I was eager to see if it could work in Dar. I also wanted to see if I could attract some Tanzanian women to be mentors, so that when I leave Dar, the vision could continue. I identified four women, three Tanzanians and an Austrian; I worked with two of the ladies, one of whom happened to go to the same church as me. The third one I met at church and the fourth I met when she had been contracted to do an event for the office. Since this was the third place that I was embarking on a Daughters programme, I spent a few months articulating the vision, the mission and the objectives, which I shared with them. The ladies were honored that I had chosen them and were very much interested in the Ministry. For nine months, we met on a monthly basis to have a clear understanding of how the mentorship programme would work. We agreed that we would work with a local university and mentor young women who were second and third year students as a way of preparing them for the world of work. We made contact with the leadership of the university and shared the vision for the programme. We received great support and interest for the programme and were a bit concerned that we would not be able to meet their expectations.

We had an initial meeting to introduce the young women to the concept and about twenty participated; we thereafter requested them to fill in a form on why they felt that such a programme would be of value to them. We then screened and shortlisted ten young women bearing in mind, that since we were all working women, we could not mentor more than two young women each. By this time, our Austrian colleague had left the country, so we found another mentor, a Tanzanian who was very much interested in the programme. We conducted training on mentorship for the mentors to ensure that we had a common understanding and then we also provided training to the mentees. When two of the mentees dropped out, that left only eight, and that meant three of the mentors each were paired with two mentees, and two mentors ended up with one each. We agreed that it was up to each one of us together with our mentees to discuss a schedule of meetings and activities, and we also held regular report back meetings to gauge our progress.

During our feedback sessions, we shared our challenges and successes. Our initial findings were that it was not possible to meet the young women more than once a month since the weekends were also reserved for family commitments; the young women were generally not forthcoming in terms of proposing meeting dates and on what they wanted to do, so the mentors had to be the ones to initiate the meetings. As we brainstormed on our findings, we concluded that maybe the young women were not very clear on the whole concept of mentorship; socio-culture factors could contribute to the fact that they did not initiate but expected things to be initiated. During one of the mentors and mentee meetings, we asked the young women to share their thoughts with us on the programme. They indicated that they were very happy to have us as mentors and that they had really benefited from the sessions. However, they also indicated that they wanted the larger meetings with other young women and not just with their mentors or other mentees. They told us that they felt that their peers would benefit from the kinds of discussions that we had planned to have with them, such as how to deal with peer pressure, poor financial management and relationships since many struggled with these issues.

Talking to the young women is always an eye opener and one learns so much from them. In hindsight, I believe that it would have been good to start with the large group meetings in order to first assess which of the young women were really committed in terms of their participation in the sessions and then to allow the trust to build between them and my colleagues and then they would have been better informed in the choice of mentor. From my experience in Geneva and Addis, I learned that it is those who consistently participate in meetings and take up specific tasks who reap the full benefit of the Daughters. Those who are bystanders and don't actually get involved or try to understand what Daughters is all about do not benefit. The Daughters of Destiny Mentorship programme continues to this day.

The interest and consistent participation of young women in the Daughters meetings attests to the fact that there is a need for such a group. Related to this point is that mentors are scarce and yet these are the people who can invest much into the lives of young women. They have gone through their trials of life and they can reach out and share their valley and mountain peak experiences. Gone are the days when aunties and older women were available to guide and lead young women on what it means to be a respected young woman. Young women face challenges in all directions and in order to 'fit in', they often bow down to peer pressure and end up losing their own identities. How many of us lost our identities and are still grappling with regaining them? It's crucial that young women be content with who they are. The programme shall remain as long as mentors are willing and available. They are not easy to come by. I sometimes think even older women lack confidence and don't believe that they can contribute meaningfully to the life of a younger woman. Some might feel overwhelmed and others are just not ready to get involved since they have to give of themselves, in terms of their time, resources and experiences, hence exposing themselves. If they have not walked through some of their own challenges, they feel that they are not in a position to mentor anyone.

The good news is that I never worry about the Daughters of Destiny Ministry because it is a work that belongs to the Lord. I just happen to be the one He has chosen to be the vision bearer and to establish groups wherever I go. He will provide helpers who are running with the vision and whatever is required for it to succeed. Providing a space where young women can discuss girl issues without any inhibitions is what they need. This is the reason why, wherever I have started the groups, I have stressed that the Daughters is not a substitute for a church youth meeting. In the meetings, I teach the young women to respect and value one another and to be open to learn from each other.

Through the Daughters groups, I have reached out to many young women and emails and texts come to me from them in different parts of the world. Responding to them all is no easy task. At the same time, it is so fulfilling to see these Daughters transformed due to some small act, such as showing them that I believe in them and care for them. This gift of mentoring is a blessing from the Lord, and to Him I am grateful. My heart is so filled with joy when I see these young women rise to heights no one ever expected. The Lord has a plan and a purpose for each one of us and the call is for each one of us to fulfill our purpose. The beauty is that as the Lord has fashioned us, and within each one of us He has deposited vital ingredients that will contribute towards our purposes being fulfilled. He molds and shapes us so that we can do what we have to with great joy and it flows naturally. It's just up to us to heed to that call.

While mentoring the young women, I have learned a great deal and just as climbing Kili, it is a humbling experience. It takes cooperation with the guide to conquer Kili. One has got to listen to the guide and trust that he knows what is best. If you have ego problems and think that you know it all, climbing Kili could prove to be fatal. In this situation, the guide knows what is best and he has the final say. When one imagines the numbers of times that they have climbed up and down the mountain, you know who is best placed to lead a novice. Being fit is no guarantee that one will conquer Kili. Several very fit people did not reach Uhuru Peak because they thought that being fit was all it would take to conquer Kili. How one acclimatizes is what counts. At the same time, being totally unfit, unhealthy and never having walked a kilometer is not going to help if one aspires to reach the summit. One of the first questions my guide asked me, was "Hopo, do you want to reach Uhuru peak?" My response was "Yes" and he said "You have got to cooperate with me and the first thing is that you need to drink two liters of water a day". I agreed and I wondered to myself, how on earth I could take in so much water. And, I am sure you know what that meant, many detours in the bushes... With the Daughters, it's so important to listen to them and just because I have lived more years than them does not mean that I have the best answers. Being a mentor is not about advising them on what to do but it's to hold their hands and guide them. It's about helping them to arrive at a place where they are content with who they are; some detours might be avoided but others they will have to face head on and decide what they want. It's about them taking responsibility for the choices that they make.

So, in conclusion, where am I today, emotionally? I am at peace with myself and I like me. It's so great to be able to say and to mean it. I like me and I am happy to spend time with me. In the past, I despised me and when I spent time alone I was putting myself down and being my own worst enemy. I surely gave myself some hard blows. Of course, there are those days when I don't like my behavior and attitude but generally, I still like me. That is me at my weakest and when I'm at that place, I need to go back and focus on the Lord. So, when those moments come lurking with negative thoughts that I am a failure and that no one really cares for me, I am reminded of the poem on pity parties. I dismiss such thoughts and begin to think of what is positive, good and admirable and then my confidence and esteem begin to soar. I realize that one has to be so conscious of what one is thinking because many times one doesn't think before one talks or one doesn't consider the implications of what one is thinking about.

Many times, my guess is that we have wrong thoughts. We reach unfounded conclusions in our minds and this is often very self destructive.

Telling you the path that my life has taken is not simple and I do not want you to think that it was in using my own strength alone that I have become the woman that I am today. I give all the glory to God and I have learned to do whatever I do with excellence. I try to give my best to everything I do and my benchmark is not another person, i.e. I don't do things to please people but to please God. His standards are excellence in all things and He empowers us to reach those levels of excellence. So whether I am washing dishes or doing a work assignment, both are done with excellence. Sometimes, I have been told that I am such a perfectionist, but that is not the truth. What I do is to strive for God's standard of excellence. I know for sure that when you excel at small things, to excel at large things is not a challenge because the character to do that has been developed and nurtured.

One question that might be crossing your mind is why I have opened myself up to share my story. One reason amongst several is to demonstrate to you that being a victim of childhood sexual abuse need not be a roadblock or prevent you from realizing your potential and dreams. I am pressing forward and I hope that you can agree with me that a positive attitude, strong will power and determination have been essential ingredients. Just as they were when I finally reached the top of Mount Kilimanjaro, so these ingredients will be important for me to finish my race well on earth. The reality is that we face many setbacks in life but if every time we fall down we can rise again, we will overcome. The many scars that negatively affect the course of our lives are inevitable but they are also reminders of how far we have come.

The issue of sexual abuse is shrouded in secrecy and we feel so ashamed of ourselves, hence we never talk about it. This was how I felt for so many years but now I know that it's not necessary to feel that way or to hide it. It has required a constant appreciation of me and it takes courage to push through, even when courage is lacking, and to learn to accept being uncomfortable because I am taking an unknown course.

My hope is that you readers who have a past of sexual abuse or who have gone through any traumatic event will be inspired and have the courage to come to terms with your painful past by opening up and disclosing your stories. Talking about it is an important step that will be so liberating and empowering as the dark sordid secret that you have never uttered to anyone is out in the open. Disclosing to the world in the first edition of this book meant that I was opening myself to all kinds of remarks and criticism, people pointing fingers at me and no doubt, I becoming a topic of discussion. I do not have any regrets because even if this book touches and changes one life, then I am content. My feeling is that being open about my experience with abuse, I will open the door for others to start dealing with the skeletons of their past and seek healing.

I have discovered that when I share my story, many victims open up and share their own experiences and in some cases I am the first person to know. As they tell their stories with much pain and tears, they admit that they feel a burden being lifted away by talking about it, because for so many years they have kept it a secret. Abuse is the common thread that links us together and allows us not to feel ashamed but rather to be relieved that someone will understand without being judgmental and critical. By sharing my story, I hope that more people realize that they are not the only ones to have gone through such agony, and that they will be encouraged to share their stories and to get the help that they need. My dream is that support groups will develop among women who have gone through sexual abuse and have been living lives of secrecy and pain. I hope that they can learn to trust others with their burdens by sharing, encouraging, and praying for each other.

Many people with whom I have shared my story have told me that they admired the fact that when I talked about what happened to me, it was as if it happened to someone else. They say that they do not sense any anger or bitterness and want to know what I did to reach that point. They want to be able to put their past behind and move forward but they say that they do not know how to do it. In this section, I will share the steps that I took, which does not mean that other ways do not exist.

1. Acknowledge, admit, and accept that you have been sexually abused, hurt, and/or rejected, and it has resulted in undesirable behavior. Come to terms with the fact that

you are a victim and that you were not responsible for and are not to blame for the abuse that was inflicted upon you. As you do some self-introspection, realize and accept that you made some bad and good choices as a result of the experience. It is very important to forgive yourself and to not allow self-blame, guilt, and condemnation to linger in your life. Start to love yourself by telling yourself how good you look every morning when you look at yourself in the mirror, even if you do not believe it. The more you keep telling yourself, the more you will begin to receive and believe it. Take Scriptures from the Bible, such as Psalm 139, which tells you how precious and valuable you are in God's sight, and keep speaking them to yourself. Then you will believe them. Don't be too hard on yourself, and remember to pamper yourself, because you are special. You need to see yourself as the Lord sees you.

2. Realize that overcoming is a daily struggle and you will have to keep challenging yourself to do the unimaginable. It's important to expand your horizons and when you face difficulties, don't give up and instead, persevere. You need to work on believing in yourself that 'you can' and not that 'you cannot' and keep saying positive things to and about yourself. Be your best cheerleader.

3. See a counselor, psychologist, pastor, or a trusted friend who will be willing to listen to you. Someone who will

allow you to be yourself, because there are times when you want to talk, but not necessarily to get advice. You want to offload and should not be pressured to say things that you would rather not. At the same time, it's important to be wary of those who want to advise and solve your problems for you. You might be advised to just forget what happened because it's easier for those who are close to you to deal with the situation. However, you must realize that you need to work through things yourself, as you see fit.

4. Take some time to be on your own, in your own quiet and favorite spot, where you can pray and/or write in a journal. As you are on your own, you will be able to articulate in all honesty what you feel and what you are going to do about those feelings. I used a combination of prayer and writing in my journal and had a new journal for every year with different themes. One was "I can do all things through Christ who strengthens me." I would give myself a Christmas present of a journal every year and I would write in it, as I felt the need. I would write letters to the Lord and express my feelings to Him. This really helped, and when I was angry with Him I would tell Him, or when I was grateful I would tell Him. Journalizing allows you to tap into your deeper reserves of creativity and problem solving. It is an inexpensive form of self-help that forces you to do something, and it gives you a chance

to see your feelings in black and white and then to make plans to do something about them. How you write is not important, just start writing as the thought comes to you. Most people resist writing in a journal because it is hard work and it so much easier to put off spending time alone. People would rather spend time watching TV, visiting friends, working, or spending time with family. The result is that you end up not knowing the real you and you don't see how to move beyond the abuse. However, journalizing is not for everyone, so just talking to the Lord as if He was in the room with you is another alternative. Whatever is on your heart, articulate it, because the Lord knows you, even more than you know yourself. Tell Him exactly what is bothering you and expose yourself to Him. Spending time alone and really getting to enjoy your own company is crucial because you have to live with yourself for the rest of your life. You cannot run away from yourself, and the sooner you realize it, the better.

5. It is important to forgive the perpetrator because anger and resentment will stand in the way and prevent you from getting ahead in your life. Bitterness builds up and is like a cancer because it eats away at you while the perpetrator's life goes ahead. The ability to forgive from the heart is one of the keys to healing for sexually abused victims. For some people, confronting the perpetrator and then forgiving him/her is not possible or easy. In my

case, it was not possible because he and his family left Lesotho and I do not know what became of them. I prayed the prayer below so that I could forgive him and release him and so that he could no longer have a hold on my life

> _____, wherever you are, I forgive you for violating my body. I hated you for what you did to me, but now I want to progress in my life, so I release you in the name of Jesus. I forgive you in the precious name of Jesus. I ask the Lord to touch you so that you can come to know His love and forgiveness, because Jesus died for each of us so that we can experience His everlasting love. May you come to know Jesus as your Lord and personal Savior. This I pray in the mighty name of Jesus. Amen.

6. Talking and sharing our experiences of sexual abuse with others who have also been abused is important. At any relevant forum, I share my experience of being sexually abused, and even though people shed a tear, they always thank me for being so courageous because they know someone else who had been abused and they wish to help them. Through sharing, it makes us realize that we are not alone in the struggle, and strength can be obtained as we encourage each other. Maybe you could start a support group in your neighborhood or church, for those

who have been abused. Of course, you might feel that you are not ready to come out into the open with your story, but given time to heal, you will probably begin to share with others as you realize that you are not alone, and it takes one courageous person to start. If you want to share your story of abuse and how you overcame, please do not hesitate to contact me. I would love to hear your story of victory, and I am sure that it will be a blessing in someone else's life.

7. Parents, if you note any sudden changes in your child's behavior—withdrawal, fear, tensing when touched—then sexual abuse cannot be ruled out. It is essential to investigate further because victims of abuse rarely disclose that they are being abused.

8. Finally, there might be one of you who would like to have a relationship with the Lord. It would be a shame for me to conclude without telling you how you can have a closer walk with the Him. You might be feeling helpless, despairing and confused, or you might have come to the point where you have tried everything to fill that void of emptiness. I came to that point and realized that Jesus might be the answer, so you might also want to invite the Lord Jesus into your life. One thing you can be sure about is that He loves you and cares for you just as you are and wants an intimate relationship with you. The Lord loves us so much that He gave His only son Jesus to die for our

sins so that we can get the gift of eternal life. All we need to do is to accept His pardon. Admitting your sinfulness, believing that Jesus died for your sins, inviting Him into your heart and life as Lord and Savior, and accepting God's forgiveness is what makes you a real Christian. The following prayer will help you do this:

> Dear God, I confess that I am a sinner and am sorry for all the wrongs that I have done. I believe that Your Son, Jesus Christ, died on the cross for my sins. Please forgive me. I invite You, Jesus, to come into my heart and life as Lord and Savior. I commit and trust my life to You. Please give me the desire to be what You want me to be and to do what You want me to do. Thank You for dying for my sins, for Your free pardon, for Your gift of eternal life, and for hearing and answering my prayer. Amen.

When you pray to receive Christ into your life, you begin a brand new spiritual life. This life needs care and nurturing, just as your physical life does. This can entail spending time in God's Word and going to a fellowship (church) where there is practical Bible teaching.

These are some of the steps that can be pursued, but this list is not exhaustive. It is only a start. Bear in mind that the idea is for us to start openly talking about sexual abuse and our painful experiences, so that we can help each other. It is only in giving of yourself or of your time, whether it is sharing your experience or spending time to listen to someone who has been traumatized, that life has the greatest fulfillment.

So, I'd like to encourage you, not only those of you who have been sexually abused but also those who have gone through some pain, suffering or any kind of injustice to join me in openly talking about your experiences.

> I would rather stumble a thousand times
> Attempting to reach a goal,
> Than to sit in a crowd
> In my weather-proof shroud,
> A shriveled and self-satisfied soul.
> I would rather be doing and daring
> All of my error-filled days,
> Than watching and waiting and dying,
> Snug in my perfect ways.
> I would rather wonder and blunder,
> Stumbling blindly ahead,
> Than for safety's sake,
> Lest I make a mistake,
> Be sure, be safe, be dead.
> - *(Author unknown)* -

For more information on the Daughters of Destiny, you can visit www.daughtersofdestinyministry.com or write to me at daughtersofdestiny@gmail.com

www.ingramcontent.com/pod-product-compliance
Lightning Source LLC
Chambersburg PA
CBHW011713290426
44113CB00019B/2663